MARK E. HEDIGER

Surviving and Thriving as a Superintendent of Schools

Leadership Lessons from Modern American Presidents

*TO MARK
I HAVE TRULY
ENJOYED BEING N*

Stephen Dlott *ONOUGH ANN
MARLBOROUGH
WORKING WITH THE
SCHOOL COMMITTEE,
THANK YOU FOR BUYING
THIS BOOK AND MOVING
ME UP A NOTCH
ON AMAZON
Steve Dlott*

ROWMAN & LITTLEFIELD EDUCATION
Lanham • New York • Toronto • Plymouth, UK

Published in the United States of America
by Rowman & Littlefield Education
A Division of Rowman & Littlefield Publishers, Inc.
A wholly owned subsidary of The Rowman & Littlefield Publishing Group, Inc.
4501 Forbes Boulevard, Suite 200, Lanham, Maryland 20706
www.rowmaneducation.com

Estover Road
Plymouth PL6 7PY
United Kingdom

British Library Cataloguing in Publication Information Available

Library of Congress Cataloging-in-Publication Data

Dlott, Stephen, 1947-
  Surviving and thriving as a superintendent of schools : leadership lessons from
modern american presidents / Stephen Dlott.
    p. cm.
  ISBN-13: 978-1-57886-513-0 (cloth : alk. paper)
  ISBN-10: 1-57886-513-1 (cloth : alk. paper)
  ISBN-13: 978-1-57886-514-7 (pbk. : alk. paper)
  ISBN-10: 1-57886-514-X (pbk. : alk. paper)
    1. School superintendents—United States. 2. School management and
organization—United States. 3. Educational leadership—United States.
I. Title.
  LB2831.72.D56 2006
  371.2'011—dc22   2006015052

$\circledcirc$^{TM} The paper used in this publication meets the minimum requirements of
American National Standard for Information Sciences—Permanence of Paper
for Printed Library Materials, ANSI/NISO Z39.48-1992.
Manufactured in the United States of America.

This book is dedicated to my wife Ann Marie. Her support and encouragement were instrumental in my completing this work.

Contents

Foreword

Perhaps a quarter of a century ago, during the years I was director of the Harvard Principals' Center, I started a writers' group for Boston-area school leaders.

It was my belief that school people carry with them an extraordinary repository of craft knowledge . . . which they have gained by virtue of working for days, months, and years in the field of public education. I am convinced that these insights of educators are at least as valuable in improving our schools as national studies, academic treatises, and endless reports.

But, alas, teachers and principals and superintendents reveal precious little to their colleagues of their wisdom acquired on the job. There are many reasons for this, of course: we may not value what we know, we may be competitors with others and not wish to disclose our "keys to the store," we may fear criticism of our efforts, or we may not know how to disclose what we know.

The writers' group attempted to help unlock and explicate, for the good of the profession and for the good of the writer, this latent, abundant craft knowledge.

Steve Dlott was a stalwart member of that writers' group. And now I have the opportunity of reading—and celebrating—what he has written.

In the engaging volume that you are about to read, you will find that he has more than fulfilled our hopes for participants in that workshop. What I believed then about school practitioners' writing I still believe.

- Put to work your lifetime experiences. You will find here a knowledge base that draws upon Steve's entire career as teacher, principal, assistant superintendent, and superintendent.
- Find your own voice. Too much of what practitioners write is an attempt to emulate academic writing: forbidding footnotes, dependent clauses, theoretical models, and "shoulds." Academic writing doesn't work very well for academics, let alone for others.

  Here you will find an engaging, distinctive, personal style that is the author's very own: thoughtful, playful, humble, and revelatory. This charmingly disarming style will warmly invite you into the superintendency, indeed, into the author's life. How many books about education have you read where the bibliography consists of stories about American presidents?
- Convey feeling. Too much writing about schools is antiseptic, devoid of the very quality that inhabitants of schools exhibit—affect. Steve Dlott's humor, hurt, anger, sadness, and delight shine through. These are qualities with which any superintendent can identify all too well. And they are qualities with which real learning is associated.
- Employ dialogue. We hear in this story of Steve Dlott's superintendency his voice. But in addition, we hear the voices of countless other educators who are players in the drama. Each one brings life, realism, energy, and affect to the story.
- Be honest. So many "autobiographies" by school leaders are inflated, self-serving, and heroic. You will find here abundant warts as well as successes. With this authenticity and transparency comes credibility. What you will soon read looks, feels, and smells the way we remember it: workload, parent involvement, stress, terror, conflict, relief, satisfaction.
- Have a unique plan. Schools and school people suffer from routinization. It's Thanksgiving, so out comes my Thanksgiving folder. Adults and students desperately need novelty. No quality does more to promote human learning.

Steve seizes upon the fruits of his insomnia in the wee hours while a school leader. During those sleepless hours, he often read biographies of U.S. presidents. He takes advantage of his background as a history teacher by inventively and skillfully juxtaposing the experiences of post–World War II presidents with his own during his superintendency. The parallels he draws are strikingly apt and successful. Lyndon Johnson's attempts to bring civil rights to America in the 1960s are very much like his own attempts to bring democratic, heterogeneously grouped classes to Westborough, Massachusetts, in the 1990s.

- Write for publication. If school leaders are going to go to all the trouble of writing their stories, and risking criticism for sharing their craft wisdom, then these stories deserve to be widely read.
- Learn from your writing. This is the work of a "reflective practitioner." By reflecting on practice, by making practice visible, one learns about practice and helps others to learn. At the conclusion of each chapter, you will find reflection points. These are the gold nuggets Steve sifts from the gravel pile of his experience. He does not leave it to the reader to figure out the "take home," the "so what?" The author is a strong proponent of "active learning." In this finely grained little volume, Steve reflects on what he has learned as he walked the walk and talked the talk as a superintendent of schools. He was then, and clearly continues to be, a leading learner.

These were among the objectives many years ago of our little writers' group. And these are the objectives I find so manifest here.

I must admit, I've never fully understood just what a school superintendent does, let alone what's behind the doing. Now I do. Enjoy your read. Learn from it. You will more than "survive the superintendency"; you will thrive on it!

Roland S. Barth
March 18, 2006

Introduction

I lay unconscious, sprawled out on the kitchen floor of my home, when my son, Michael, discovered me at 4:30 a.m. "Mom, come quick! Something is very wrong with Dad," he shouted to my wife, who was in bed asleep. Ann Marie saw my prostrate body and immediately called 911. The next thing I knew, I was being strapped to a stretcher and led out of my house by two burley firefighters. I became more alert as I felt snow melting against my face while they carried me across my front lawn into the waiting ambulance. From the glare of the flashing lights and all the commotion in the early morning, I suspect my neighbors thought I had died.

When I reached Memorial Hospital ten minutes later, I was rushed into the emergency room. The attending physician examined me, smiled, and said, "Mr. Dlott, there is nothing wrong with you except that you are dehydrated. You had merely fainted."

What a start to my career as a superintendent of schools. That morning had been my first major public decision, and it involved whether I cancelled school due to snow conditions. The fact that I had never before made this type of call only added to my anxiety. While at the breakfast table, I had been reviewing the pros and cons of each course of action when I passed out. All I could now think about was what had

I gotten myself into when I accepted the job as superintendent of schools in Westborough, Massachusetts. Perhaps I would have been far better off if I had remained an assistant superintendent or returned to the principalship. Certainly, with all this anxiety, I did not appear destined to be the next Horace Mann.

More decisions quickly followed. However, I knew I was getting better because I remained conscious during all these trying ordeals. Contentious meetings with the finance committee, a public dispute over where to site the new high school, and the closing of a primary school for air-quality issues all added to the daily stress of the position. A low point in my career occurred when an irate parent pointed an accusing finger at me at a public meeting about air quality in the schools and said, "Dr. Dlott, you have betrayed the children of Westborough." Hey, who did this woman think I was, Benedict Arnold? I thought that I done a good job on that issue, and here I was being flogged at a public forum.

Controversy only motivated me to work harder. The steady diet of stress began to affect my sleeping. I would wake up totally alert each morning at 2:00 a.m. I decided that instead of tossing and turning, I would get out of bed and do two hours of paperwork. I reasoned I could complete my work, then go back to bed, and still get a total of seven hours sleep each night. The extra work time did allow me to generate additional letters and reports at a rapid rate. Unfortunately, I became more sluggish during the day, and the workload continued to increase.

As an escape from the daily turmoil, during the quiet of late evening hours after members of my family were asleep, I took refuge in reading presidential biographies. I was relaxed while reading about other people's problems rather than just experiencing my own. I came to the conclusion that all leaders undergo stress as it is an occupational hazard. It was a comfort for me to read how pressure affected our country's presidents. Harry Truman became exasperated as our nation's chief executive due to the lack of cooperation from Congress, stinging criticism by the press, and low ratings from the public on national opinion polls. As the pressure increased, Truman considered not running for reelection as he finished out the final months of his first term. Prior to the 1948 election, he had outlined for Dwight Eisenhower a scenario in which he, Harry Truman, would step down to become a vice presidential candidate if General Eisenhower would agree to run as president on the

Democratic ticket. This scenario never came to fruition, and Truman narrowly won reelection that year, while Eisenhower won the presidency four years later as a Republican.

Eisenhower's vice president, Richard Nixon, unsuccessfully sought the presidency in 1960 before being elected in 1968. While in the Oval Office, he became so distraught by the public criticism, he reportedly began talking to the portraits of former presidents in his office. I felt a certain self-assuredness knowing that I had never thought of doing that.

Even a man as physically and mentally tough as Lyndon Johnson became worn down by the pressures of the Oval Office. Pictures of former president Johnson, a man who had previously weathered many brutal battles in the Senate, reveal a man who appeared to age ten years during his five years in office. Maybe it wasn't I. Maybe the ordeal of a superintendent of schools, with its high visibility, is comparable on a very small scale to the demands of being president of the United States. Both jobs require individuals to respond to very exacting demands from many constituencies, often at great personal sacrifice of time and energy while being severely criticized.

My reading of presidential vulnerability also made me more confident in my ability, even in areas like finance, where I knew I had room for improvement. I never enjoyed finance, and as a superintendent, I dreaded the tedium of the budget-building process. I smiled when I read in Richard Reeve's biography of John F. Kennedy that President Kennedy had made light of his own inadequacies in the field of economics. After he was elected to the House of Representatives, Kennedy went for economics tutoring at American University. He quickly lost interest and stopped attending class. He joked that when his instructor at American heard that he, Jack Kennedy, had been elected president of the United States, he had probably jumped out a window.

This book is about leadership. It draws lessons from the administrations of eight modern presidents and applies those lessons to the superintendency. The book is in no way intended to evaluate or rate the presidents. Rather, its purpose is to share leadership strategies with superintendents through reflections on presidential actions, as well as on my own experiences. Whenever I have related incidents from my career, I have frequently changed the names of people and locations in order to preserve anonymity for acquaintances who may feel I might have been unfair in my description of them.

As you read this book, please keep one thing in mind: as a superintendent of schools, you are a leader. You had the courage to apply for the job, to leave a secure position, and to take responsibility for the direction of a school system. You are willing to take the risk of being "out there" for all types of criticisms. The fact that you come in every day and do your best is a testimony to your dedication, commitment, and courage. You, along with every other superintendent, subscribe to the belief that you work for the benefit of children. "If you can't stand the heat, get out of the kitchen" is a famous quote often attributed to former president Harry Truman. You have chosen a path less traveled, and you have stayed in the kitchen in spite of the heat.

CHAPTER ONE

Terminating Ineffective Administrators

"I'm doing it for the kids. I'm doing it for the kids." Reminiscent of a Buddhist monk, I recite this mantra repeatedly in my mind whenever I decide not to renew the contract of a principal in my district. Let's face it: in school administration jargon, nonrenewal is a euphemism for dismissal as the principal has little recourse except to look for a position in another school system. Personally, I find it disheartening when I am compelled to terminate the employment of a loyal, decent human being who is doing his best, and I hope I never find this task easy. However, to paraphrase an old maxim, a superintendent has got to do what a superintendent has got to do. Like you, my first responsibility is to the students in the school system. Ineffective administrators must either improve or be replaced.

The nonrenewal conference is agony. This is not like the National Football League, where a messenger, known as the Turk, alerts a player that he is to be cut from the team's roster with the words, "Hey, coach wants to see you, and bring your playbook." Rather my termination conference with an administrator is a one-on-one uncomfortable moment of truth. I am usually filled with guilt and remorse during this type of conference as I always wonder if I have done enough to help my lieutenant. After all, the principals are our field commanders as we direct our school system from central office, a place in which students and teachers are noticeably absent. We count on the principals to carry out systemwide goals and to garner faculty and community support for district initiatives. Principals also advise us and provide information that not only helps us to make better decisions but also allows us to be more informative to the school board and the entire community.

On a personal level, we often know the principal's spouse and children, and we sometimes have even been invited to family functions. This personal relationship makes severance all the more difficult. Sure, it is easy if the principal has committed a crime or is totally incompetent. However, this is seldom the case. Instead, what prompts the action of dismissal is that the principal is not providing the necessary leadership in the building. By the time I finally realize that the problem is not solvable, there are already serious issues manifested in the school, which are usually accompanied by low faculty morale and parent dissatisfaction.

At the final conference, what I find most uncomfortable is having to deny the inevitable request from the principal for more time to work out the issues. In order to end the painful discussion and get closure, my final comment is, "I'd be happy to write you a reference." What an empty offer. What can I really say? "He is a great principal, not nearly good enough to remain in my district, but he would be dynamite in yours."

I actually do work hard to assist the principal in securing another position, and I have been quite successful, which has eased my personal pangs of conscience. Realistically, dismissing ineffective principals goes with the job of superintendent of schools, and managers in all professions face similar dilemmas. There are lessons superintendents can learn from the manner in which America's thirty-third president, Harry Truman, eventually relieved General Douglas MacArthur from command during the Korean War.

Support for Subordinates

The Korean War began on June 25, 1950, when the North Korean Army attacked South Korea. President Harry Truman quickly decided that he could not allow this outright act of aggression to go unchallenged by the United States, or all countries in Asia would be at risk of attack.

While contemplating a course of action, Truman received advice to replace America's Far Eastern military commander, the seventy-year-old Douglas MacArthur. The aging general was viewed by many highly placed people in Washington as too difficult to work with due to his abrasive and egotistical manner. However, Truman was too smart to succumb to this pressure. To fire the still-competent MacArthur would have created a firestorm in the country. Douglas MacArthur was not just another military officer. In the minds of most Americans, he was a legitimate American hero. MacArthur was a highly decorated five-star general who had received the Congressional Medal of Honor for "gallantry and intrepidity at the risk of life above and beyond the call of duty." He had commanded the allied forces in the Pacific that crushed the Japanese war machine during World War II. Later, he further distinguished himself in peace time as military governor of Japan, where he helped to create a democratic constitution for that nation. He certainly was no easy target.

President Truman made the decision to work with MacArthur rather than to immediately recall or demote him. A president plays to a national audience, and by giving the distinguished general the opportunity to again lead American forces, Truman not only kept a still very capable general in charge during a critical period, but he also made an astute move politically.

My Douglas MacArthur was a six-foot, portly, middle school principal named Michael Swift. We hired Mike through the traditional route of an interview, with a screening committee composed of teachers, parents, and administrators, followed by a site visit and reference checks, before confirmation by me. "Steve, this guy has a clear vision of what a middle school should be," gushed the chair of the screening committee. The rest of the committee nodded enthusiastically. "He can definitely provide the leadership that we need in Westborough."

I couldn't wait to meet this middle school messiah. Westborough's recent transition from a traditional two-year junior high school to a three-year, child-centered middle school had been very contentious with a reluctance on the part of some teachers and a retiring principal to embrace the new model. Some of the older staff blamed overprotective parents for pushing the middle school concept to promote a more nurturing environment. These teachers complained that this new child-centered approach would compromise academic standards. However, the message from the school board and the community, which I supported enthusiastically, was, Build us a quality middle school, now.

Mike's interview with me was equally impressive. He used all the right terms: child-centered environment, heterogeneous grouping, advisor-advisee, interdisciplinary study, enhanced parent communication, and the prominence of the team as the backbone of a middle school. I could not have orchestrated better responses. In addition, he came from a highly performing school district in suburban Hartford, Connecticut. To me, this was a huge plus as I view people coming from a high-achieving system as an asset to Westborough as they frequently bring new ideas with them. I always remember the words of famed Boston Celtics basketball coach Red Auerbach, who said that he liked to draft players from winning college teams as they know what it takes to win.

Mike Swift was also an active member of the New England League of Middle Schools and served on many of their committees. Surely his circle of contacts would translate into speakers for the faculty and possibly grants for the district. Mike appeared to me to be the perfect candidate to unite the faculty. Little did I realize that they would later unite in a revolution against his leadership.

Administrators usually get a brief honeymoon following appointment as people try to cooperate at the outset to make the system work. Mike's honeymoon period proved short-lived. At the opening day meeting with the faculty, Mike Swift came on too strong with his commitment to a middle school philosophy. He told the faculty that they were fine, dedicated teachers but were being too resistant to change. He stressed that, to make the middle school work effectively, they must make a philosophical conversion to adopt a less rigid and more humanistic approach in order to address the needs of the whole child. Michael Swift was not wrong in many of the things he was saying. Certain middle school staff members did need to demonstrate more flexibility in their approach with students. However, the faculty understood the message to be, Lighten up on the academic rigor to placate the parents.

A lot of things improved in that first year. We finally had a visible principal, committed to middle school, who was literally all over the building, working with students and teachers. He was also very approachable and would demonstrate sensitivity to staff in one-on-one situations. The parents and students appeared to like him in spite of an undercurrent of faculty criticism. I, too, was pleased with the direction of the school. Our middle school teams were becoming stronger, and the new interdisciplinary units were impressive. In fact, after only his second year, we were invited to the New England League of Middle Schools Conference to present our programs. I took pride in describing to the school board how well the transition to middle school was progressing. At these meetings, I would announce the names of other Massachusetts schools that were visiting us as they developed their own middle schools. Of course, I did hear some criticism of Mike's management style from the staff. My attitude was, Hey, let a few negative teachers grouse; positive things were happening.

It was in groups that Mike encountered his greatest difficulty. He would advocate collective decision making but would react defensively when suggestions were made. Mike defined consensus as everyone agreeing with him. It became so contentious that he would storm out of meetings, saying to people, "You don't understand." The faculty first found this disconcerting but eventually came to view it as comical. I was approached by some of the senior members of the faculty with the message that this principal was not a good match for our school. In spite of their opposition, I supported the beleaguered principal. My attitude was that my job is to work with the principal and support change. I felt it would be wrong for me to order a retreat as soon as a principal began to take a risk. Also, quickly reining in an enthusiastic principal would send a chilling message to the other administrators in the district.

Goal Setting

What would President Truman have done? He certainly worked hard with General MacArthur to keep communications open. Truman's greatest concern at the outset of the Korean War was that the war would expand from a small regional war into a large-scale global conflict. America had only recently finished participating in World War II, and

Truman was not interested in another huge military confrontation. What made the situation even more dangerous was that nuclear weapons were now a reality in the American and Russian military arsenals. In order to make it clear to MacArthur that he did not want the conflict to escalate into World War III, Harry Truman sent his special envoy, Averill Harriman, to Japan with a message for General MacArthur. The message set forth two diplomatic goals:

1. Avoid any action that might provoke a third world war.
2. Do not antagonize the Chinese Communist government by publicly supporting Chiang Kai-Shek, the leader of the Nationalist Chinese.

Although MacArthur agreed to be a good soldier and to follow the president's wishes, he actually did the opposite. One week after Harriman's visit, MacArthur wrote a speech to the Veterans of Foreign Wars in which he stated that we should not appease the Chinese Communists, and we should certainly stand behind Chiang Kai-Shek and defend Formosa in the event of an attack by the Chinese Communists. MacArthur was being MacArthur, independent and difficult.

Goal setting also appeared to me to be a reasonable strategy to assist an embattled principal. After all, this approach had worked well for me in the past with principals who were encountering difficulty. However, like Truman, I found out that this strategy is not always successful. Sometime administrators are too strong-minded to work with their supervisors.

"Let's keep it simple," I stressed to Mike. "You have only two goals for the upcoming school year: engage the faculty in productive dialogue about the direction of the middle school and listen to their suggestions, and continue to develop a quality middle school."

"Mike you just can't do this alone," I told him. "You must work with the faculty to develop a collective vision so everyone feels a part of the process."

Mike smiled and said, "I'm with you on this one, boss. No more unilateral decisions."

As he said it, all I could think of was the lyric of the old song that went, "Your lips tell me no, no, but there is yes, yes in your eyes."

Directives

Truman continued to experience frustration with his recalcitrant general. Still, MacArthur demonstrated his genius as a military tactician when he deployed American forces behind the invading North Korean Army, trapping them between two armies and cutting off their supply route. The North Koreans began retreating back to their own country. Apparently, the old commander still had tricks up his sleeve as he appeared to justify President Truman's faith in him.

With Truman's permission, American troops drove into North Korea recording stunning success. However, when American forces approached the North Korean–Chinese border, the Chinese Communist Army entered the war and drove back the Americans into South Korea; only the keen military planning of General Mathew Ridgeway prevented a complete rout. General MacArthur was stung by the severe criticism of his military leadership by reporters who blamed him for the sudden reversal of fortune. MacArthur told the reporters that he could have certainly defeated the Communist forces if Washington had only not tied his hands in the drafting of military strategy. The general made it clear that total victory could only be assured if he could expand the war and attack China.

President Truman was outraged by MacArthur's overstepping his authority in questioning the policy of the president of the United States. He sent a directive to all military offices that press releases had to be cleared with the Department of State before being issued. Certainly, this directive was aimed at the outspoken Far Eastern commander. It was now becoming obvious to Harry Truman that MacArthur had to be replaced.

A written directive is a strong message. As superintendent, I only use this technique if reasoning with a principal has not been productive. A directive means that I don't trust the judgment of a subordinate, and I want to tell him how to handle a situation in a certain way. I encourage principals to argue with me privately and to vigorously advocate their own positions on issues. However, as superintendent, I am the administrative leader of the system, and I expect, at the end of our debates, that principals will work cooperatively with me. When an administrator doesn't show the ability to be a team player and support district initiatives, he or she loses my confidence, as General MacArthur lost the confidence of President Truman.

I recall vividly an incident in which I had to issue a directive to middle school principal Mike Swift because he was not following the direction of the school system. I had received a complaint from a parent that an eighth-grade English teacher, Sue Johnson, would not allow her students to write their first drafts of writing assignments on a computer. This surprised me as integration of technology into the writing process was a systemwide goal, and teachers were to encourage students to draft and to edit essays on computer. Westborough had spent thousands of dollars to support this concept, and the school board and the entire administration were committed to this approach. As this parent complaint was a building issue, I referred the mother back to the teacher and Mike. However, she said she had already contacted both of these people and received no satisfaction. The mother said Mike was very courteous but did not appear to listen at all to her point of view. What frightened me most was that I was not the least bit surprised by her statement.

I immediately met with Mike to hear his side of the story.

"What this mother says is true," Mike admitted. "Sue Johnson does not accept homework essays generated on a computer. She has this fear that some parents may actually type into the computer their student's document, then edit the paper with grammar and spell-check, while the students gain little from the assignment."

"Mike, that is ridiculous. Parents can edit handwritten homework now, and we'd never know. What is the difference?"

"I agree. I certainly do support the systemwide goal of integrating computers in the writing process. All my other English teachers have bought into the technique. Sue is a really good teacher, and she just needs time. Remember, you're the one who says I have to listen to teachers," he reminded me. "Well I listened to Sue, and for now I support her."

There is something about having your own words thrown back in your face that is truly annoying.

"Mike, time to accept change is fine, but this initiative has been in place for almost three years, and you have been vocal in your support for the concept at every principals' meeting." I could feel my voice getting louder and more irritated. I was now lecturing instead of discussing. "Also, listening does not imply automatic agreement. Rather, as the instructional leader, you are responsible for the instructional practices in your building."

"I agree," he reiterated. I was beginning to tire of that phrase as it sounded patronizing. Mike Swift now appeared to me to be passive aggressive. I could now clearly see why Mike angered people. He really had trouble understanding the position of others. He kept rigidly making the same point: "My goal for the year is to listen to the faculty before setting direction."

"Mike, input is important, but how about your second goal, developing a quality middle school? How can you have a quality program if some students do not get the benefit of what we think is the best educational approach?"

I had now had enough. The conversation was going nowhere, and I decided to end it. "Listen, Mike, if you are uncomfortable telling Sue to allow the use of technology in developing essays, I would be happy to do so. However, I am directing you to make sure our systemwide writing initiative is implemented in all English classrooms in this building."

What shocked me was that Mike thought it was a fine idea for me to confront Mrs. Johnson. Maybe he was relieved that I would be the one who assumed this task, and he could be "the good guy" who stood up for one of his teachers against the superintendent. Certainly, he could use a public relations boost with the faculty. Still, with his position on the matter, he was not convincing me of his leadership ability. Why would I need him if I had to go to his school to speak with one of his teachers?

Termination

President Truman was also experiencing frustration with his recalcitrant subordinate as the war dragged on and casualties increased. In March of 1951, MacArthur was outraged when he learned that Truman planned to propose a peace settlement with the Communist Chinese to end hostilities. General MacArthur decided that he would strike first and immediately called a press conference. He publicly declared that the Chinese Army must surrender to him personally or be destroyed.

Truman was flabbergasted by the disloyalty of his commander and issued a reprimand. The die was now cast. The final straw was when Representative Joe Martin, the Republican majority leader in the House of Representatives, read a letter from MacArthur on the floor of the House. The letter, contrary to policy of the president of the United States, advocated expanding the war by attacking Communist China and unleashing the nationalist forces of Chiang Kai-Shek against the Communist enemy. That was it. Amid a cry of outrage from the country, President Harry Truman dismissed Douglas MacArthur from his command.

In my own situation, conditions continued to deteriorate at the middle school. Complaints about Mike Swift's leadership and his poor decision making continued to flow into central office from teachers and parents. I do believe Mike was honestly trying to turn the situation around. However, he faced the obstacle of having lost the trust of both the faculty and the parents.

I was by now totally frustrated with his lack of leadership skills, and I too had lost faith in him as a principal. Mike's contract was not renewed. The reason I gave him was that, although he had made a significant contribution to improving the school, because of his management style, he was not capable of providing the leadership that we needed at our middle school. I also told him that the school system wanted to move in another direction. What that actually means, I still don't know, but it sounded appropriate at the time. However, we both knew he was just not the right person for the position.

Results

When a staff member is terminated, there will usually be supporters of that person who are outraged. In the case of President Truman, there was a firestorm of criticism nationwide when he dismissed General Douglas MacArthur from his command. When the general returned to the United States, he received a huge ticker tape parade in Manhattan, where people lined the streets to cheer the old war hero. MacArthur even addressed a joint session of Congress, where he received thunderous applause.

Truman's popularity at this point with the American public was very low as people tended to blame him for the length of the war and the lack of results. Many viewed the dismissing of MacArthur as one more example of the president's poor judgment. Still, in spite of short-term criticism, history has judged President Truman a true leader, and one of the reasons is that he kept the military from assuming policy judgments that should only be made by the president. In the ranking of presidents in our nation's history, Truman is regarded as one of the truly effective presidents in American history.

In Westborough, the dismissal of Mike Swift was far easier, and there certainly was no mention of parades or speeches in his honor. Few people expressed sadness at his departure. Still, I had felt badly because Mike had worked hard and actually made some significant contributions to the development of a quality middle school in Westborough. Shortly afterwards, a new principal was hired who continued to improve the quality of our middle school.

Reflection Points

- Work jointly with principals to establish clear goals and expectations. Each principal should understand the direction of the school system and his role as a school leader.
- Be honest and straightforward in discussing concerns. It is important that administrators know as early as possible if there are issues that must be addressed. Do not sugarcoat the message, or the importance of the message may be diluted.
- New administrators need time to adjust to your school system. It is critical to their success that you work closely with them to understand district priorities, procedures, and culture.
- Utilize mentors to assist principals who can benefit from additional coaching. Mentors can provide a nonthreatening approach for improvement.
- Be supportive of a principal who may not have been a good match for your school system. However, when you refer that individual to another superintendent, you must always be forthcoming and truthful concerning strengths and weaknesses of the principal.

Professionalism demands that you not merely pass your problems on to another school system.

- Concern for children has a higher priority than personal loyalty. When an administrator does not demonstrate effectiveness or potential for improvement, he must not be allowed to continue in your school system.

CHAPTER TWO

―⚬⚬⚬―

Decision Making

"Decisions R Us" could well be the motto of every superintendent of schools in the United States. Few professions require our rapid-fire and nerve-wracking pace of decision making. The emotional nature of the issues we confront guarantees a steady diet of stress. Unlike a manager of a major corporation like General Motors, whose goal is to capture only a share of consumers in the car market, we superintendents try to please everyone, as even one disgruntled parent can create enough controversy to put us on the front page of the local newspaper. Okay, I may be paranoid, but sometimes, when a parent that I don't know walks into a school board meeting, I say to myself, Why is he here? Is this an angry parent about to go for my jugular?

In selecting our profession, we all knew that the superintendency would involve the challenges and pressures related to curriculum development, school law, instructional leadership, personnel administration, and school finance. These were the topics that we studied in graduate school. However, how many of us realized that some of our most nagging parental concerns would revolve around such mundane issues as

- Why can't sixth graders have dances?
- Why can't you people lighten up a little on homework? The way the teachers load up the fourth-grade book bags, every kid in this school walks like Quasimodo.
- Why can't I choose my child's teachers?

This is not to discount the importance of these types of issues as they can become emotionally charged in the community. Still, none of these topics is the reason why we chose to become superintendents. We chose our profession to make a difference in the lives of children.

When I first became a superintendent, I feared the ramifications of my decisions, which made me tentative in making calls. I was cautious as I wanted people to agree with my solutions and think me wise. The old adage among superintendents in the area was, A superintendent is only as good as his last snow call. Given that New England winters are unpredictable, that saying did not give me any degree of comfort. I was especially concerned with the reactions of the school board. I wanted its members to feel confident that they had made a sound choice when they promoted me from within the system to be superintendent rather than looking outside the district for candidates.

My initial decisions tended to be political. I confused the concepts of loyalty and leadership. I would unnecessarily call school board members on a regular basis to explain my decisions. This did help me develop a great rapport with the school board members, but I wasted valuable time and energy that I could have devoted to pressing educational issues. Even worse, it created an unnecessary dependence on my part, which was neither healthy nor in the best interest of the school system. My closeness to committee members even extended to the point where once, when my wife had to work late, I called the chair of the school board to ask for advice about the best method to cook a chicken. Her recipe was delicious, and the dinner turned out wonderfully. However, I soon found myself questioning whether I was leading the school board, or whether the school board was leading me.

With experience came confidence in my own ability and fewer calls to school board members. One area of decision making that I found most unproductive was the approval of personal days. On occasion, I would call teachers into my office to discuss what were sometimes very personal family issues ranging from attending a parent conference for their own child to caring for a sick mother. After these discussions, I would invariably grant the request. Today, unless the personal day request is for a vacation extension, I automatically grant it. It is just not important enough for me to spend the time to force a staff member into a position where they have to explain to me how important it is to take a day to attend a wedding out of state or to watch their child in a soccer tournament in New Hampshire. These conversations waste valuable administrative time, as well as create an unnecessary adversarial situation with the teacher.

In my mind, my position on personal days comes down to two things: First, the overwhelming number of personal day requests are legitimate, and I am not sure, without hiring the services of a private investigator, that I could siphon off marginal requests. Second, I like to believe that besides being a fine superintendent, I am a good person who cares about people. I do not want written on my gravestone

Here lies the man who enforced the strictest possible interpretation of contractual language.
God rest his soul.
His final request was that no teachers be given personal time to attend his funeral.

I have also become adept at remanding decisions to where they should be made rather than trying to solve all problems. If parents have trouble with a teacher, they should see that teacher, then the principal, before seeing me. A parent who complains that football practice is too demanding is referred to the coach or the athletic director. Bus complaints are referred to the bus coordinator. All concerned parents are informed that I would be happy to sit with them once they have gone through proper channels and discussed the matter with those best able to resolve the issue. I want to dispel the belief that it is best to start at the top.

The decisions that I retain in my domain often involve appeals of other administrative rulings, school-system finances, policy issues, emergencies, staffing, and decisions that have a long-term impact on the school system, such as curriculum design and strategic planning. When enrollment growth compelled Westborough to construct a third primary school, I was faced with a decision that all superintendents dread: how do I redistrict the town's primary schools? The redistricting issue focused on whether the three schools should be neighborhood schools or whether the districts should be configured so that each school reflected the ethnic mix of the entire town. The model for this decision could well have been President Dwight David Eisenhower's decision concerning American military involvement in Vietnam.

Review Background

In order to understand critical issues, a leader must study the background of the situations he faces. As a former general with extensive foreign policy experience, Dwight Eisenhower knew well the history of Vietnam. In 1954 the French were fighting to maintain their colonial empire by retaining possession of Indochina (Vietnam, Cambodia, and Laos) through military force. Without a program to move these countries toward independence, the French strategy appeared to President Eisenhower to be shortsighted, especially in Vietnam. France's military adversary in Vietnam, the Vietminh Communist guerillas, appeared to be winning overwhelmingly the hearts and minds of the Vietnamese people.

The French, on the other hand, were viewed by the people as colonial masters. As a result of a large number of small night raids by the Vietminh guerillas, the French military was incurring increasing casualties. The enemy appeared invisible to the French since, during the day, Vietminh fighters easily blended in with the rest of the Vietnamese population following their attacks. A large French force eventually became surrounded at Dien Bien Phu, a mountainous region near the Laotian border, and the French begged for American armed intervention. The question was what Eisenhower would do.

While in Westborough, I was aware of the thirty-year rivalry between the parents in the two elementary schools, which spanned my administration and that of the five prior superintendents. Westborough had been a small, quiet town until a building boom began in the 1970s and 1980s and continued into the early 1990s. In the Lincoln school district, on the east side of town, three large apartment complexes were built, as were a number of newer homes, during this time. On the west side of town, which comprised the Jefferson school district, many more single-family housing developments were constructed, which contained very expensive homes. In the Jefferson district, there were no multifamily dwellings. Enrollments soared at both schools. Lincoln enrolled a socioeconomically mixed group of students, including a significant number from families who spoke limited English and who lived primarily in the apartments, which are located on a major roadway on the outskirts of town. Meanwhile, more and more children of affluent parents moved into Jefferson. Lincoln parents became increasingly concerned that the education in the two schools was not equal. Some mockingly called Jefferson Elementary School "the academy."

There was anger and cynicism as Jefferson student achievement scores on standardized tests outpaced Lincoln students'. A constant concern among Lincoln School parents was whether their children were at a disadvantage because the limited-English-speaking minority children were slowing down the rate of learning in the classrooms at Lincoln. This became a third rail in school board discussions. As the school board representatives were usually equally divided between the Lincoln and Jefferson districts, no superintendent chose to make this an issue.

When a third elementary school was approved in Westborough because of enrollment growth in the town, redistricting became a public debate. People were concerned that the new school district, which would encompass the older sections of Westborough and a large apartment complex, would be like Lincoln and have a significant number of minority students, while Jefferson would continue to be an enclave of affluence. The number-one issue in Westborough was whether the schools should be redistricted on neighborhood lines or the new map should be gerrymandered to allow for non-English-speaking students and students from the apartments to be equally distributed among the three schools. As the leader of the school system, I received calls from residents on both sides of this issue. Where did I stand? I didn't even know.

Review Core Values

In making an important decision it is best to review your own core values. Unfortunately, most issues are not black and white. Even core values can be in conflict. Dwight Eisenhower found himself in that predicament. President Eisenhower valued democracy, and he saw the Communists as threatening world domination. He witnessed firsthand the Russian deceit at Yalta in 1945 where Soviet leaders had spoken of peace only to later forcefully dominate smaller countries in Eastern Europe as satellites. He viewed communism as the enemy of democracy with its purpose being to impose its economic system and totalitarian form of government in countries around the world. He did not wish to be seen as the president who sat passively and watched the take over of Vietnam.

On the other hand, President Eisenhower knew that committing American forces to a war in Vietnam could lead to war with China and possibly the Soviet Union. As commander-in-chief of Allied forces in Europe during World War II, he knew the horrors of war, and he had little desire to plunge America into what could become another world conflict. He was aware that the age of the conventional war might well be over, and the next world war could be nuclear.

Dwight Eisenhower also hated colonialism. The French continually suppressed the Vietnamese desire for independence. In his own mind, how could he justify helping France continue to subjugate the Vietnamese people? Both his aversion to another war and his distaste for colonialism weighed heavily against intervention. A part of him wanted to help the French militarily, while another part feared the consequences of intervention.

In my situation, I also had to clarify and prioritize my own values in redistricting. I like to look at myself as a champion of the underdog, and I like to believe that this value is at the center of my being. Most of us tend to view ourselves in that way. As a doctoral candidate many years ago, my dissertation conducted in Bridgeport and Hartford, Connecticut, was on Latino students, and I felt it helped give me sensitivity for students who are culturally diverse. In any position I have held, I have always strived to have my district respect diversity. Initially, I had difficulty even considering the concept of busing minority children because they were not welcome by some people in their neighborhood school. However, I was to learn that there were many persuasive arguments on the other side. Conversely, I also valued the input of the community. After all, people in the Lincoln district who wanted to relocate the minority students among three schools were not a bunch of bigots. Instead, they were expressing sincere views concerning their children's education, and the concept of equity in the school system. They were correct when they said that children with limited English proficiency do present difficult challenges to classroom teachers. Equity in the district's schools is also a core value for me. In addition, I also agreed with them that minority students' attending Jefferson would be a definite asset for that school and should be taken into consideration.

Solicit Input

Important decisions should be made carefully, with all sides of the issue being explored. Eisenhower was a good listener. He had proved that as a military commander during World War II. He was able to work effectively with generals with difficult personalities, such as George Patton, Bernard Montgomery, and Charles de Gaulle, in developing military strategy. He was a patient and reflective listener, and he had a reputation for bringing people together. However, on this issue of military intervention, there was no middle ground. Either the United States would intervene militarily in Vietnam on the side of the French, or it would not intervene.

Within his own administration, there was an advocacy group that advised strong action to combat communism in Vietnam. This group was led by Chairman of the Joint Chiefs of Staff Admiral Arthur Radford and Secretary of State John Foster Dulles. They believed that at some point the United States would have to take a military stand against the forces of communism. They reasoned that it was better to fight communism now while we still had nuclear superiority. They further stressed that any capitulation to the Communists by the United States would cause democracies all over the world to lose confidence in America's resolve to confront military aggression.

The pro-interventionist advocates justified their position with the domino theory. According to that theory, if Vietnam fell, then other countries would also fall to insurgency. Cambodia, Laos, Malaysia, Indonesia, Burma, and even Japan could be vulnerable to takeover. This scenario pointed to the possible loss of the entire Asian continent.

Eisenhower also heard from many of his military comrades from World War II who were now the leaders of France. They urged him not to let Dien Bien Phu fall. They begged him for aerial support to defeat the encircling Vietminh. They needed pilots, planes, bombs, and possibly nuclear weapons. It is never easy to say no to old friends who look to you for help.

The president also had many advisors, such as Secretary of the Army General Matthew Ridgeway, a hero of the Korean War, who passionately urged against using American forces in Vietnam. Ridgeway and others of the same views in the Eisenhower administration and in the Congress saw Vietnam as the possible beginning of a new world war. To defeat Vietnam, they reasoned, would necessitate bombing Communist China, which provided the Vietminh with supplies. This type of action could bring the Soviet Union into the war. Many war critics also were firmly convinced that aerial support for the French would not be enough. Eventually, American troops would have to be committed, and we would be ensnared in a giant Asia land war. Ridgeway and other war critics believed Vietnam was just not worth the risk. The American people were also divided, with a strong desire to fight Communists on one hand and an equally strong, or perhaps stronger, desire not to experience another world war.

Like Eisenhower, I was lobbied by advocates of two conflicting positions. One group centered on Lincoln parents felt that the elementary schools must be balanced by minority representation. In their view, Jefferson Elementary School should enroll minority students, even if these students had to drive by the new school during their commute to Jefferson, and even if students in some Jefferson neighborhoods had to drive by their neighborhood school to attend the new school. "It is only fair that there should be minority balance in each school reflecting the town's ethnic mixture," they contended. If all schools had approximately the same proportional ethnic mix, they reasoned, than one school would not always be at a disadvantage by having a large number of students who could not speak English in their classrooms.

On the other side of the issue were many people on the West Side whose children attended Jefferson Elementary School. They believed that primary schools should be neighborhood schools. These people believed that transporting students out of their neighborhood would merely result in a longer bus ride and relocation to an unfamiliar environment, which was not in the best interests of the children. When you are not sure what to do, and the politics is intense, it may be wise to solicit input from within the community. I established a study group composed of teachers, parents from both Jefferson and Lincoln schools, and administrators to review the issue. I also conducted group meetings with teachers, focus groups with parents, and a community forum with the public. Although reaction in each group was mixed, the majority of each group favored balancing the schools to reflect the town's social and cultural composition. Most people who attended these meetings appeared to be tired of fighting for so many years concerning the equity issue. However, one notable exception was the parents from the Sherwood, our largest apartment complex, with a heavy concentration of minorities. They made it clear in a letter signed by all of the parents in the apartment complex that they did not want their children bused away from their neighborhood school merely because they were minorities. These parents felt that treating their children differently from other Westborough children would stigmatize them in the eyes of the community. Their concerns were understandable because in many of the balancing plans, Sherwood children would go to Jefferson.

Evaluate Alternatives

Eisenhower was in a difficult situation. There were two options. He could attempt to draw the line in the sand to stop communism by aiding the French through American air power. To stand up to the Communists then might stop a potential overrun of all Southeast Asia at a later date. The old warrior and strong anti-Communist could well see the reason for war. He saw communism as a threat, and he now had a chance to confront it. The United States had the overwhelming military superiority, which would not last forever. If we were going to stop the Communists, then this was the time to do it.

His second option was just to do nothing further to back up the French and to let Dien Bien Phu fall. The United States could then watch for what could be salvaged at the peace conference already scheduled for Geneva. The consequences of that option would be that if Vietnam fell to the Communists, the dominoes might begin to fall. In that scenario, the United States as a country and Eisenhower as a leader might be perceived as weak, which could result in further Communist aggression.

My two options were certainly easier than President Eisenhower's. Option one was simply to redistrict the Sherwood students to Jefferson. This would balance the minority student population, which had caused so much controversy for so long. However, it would require that Sherwood children be driven past their neighborhood school to attend Jefferson while certain students in the Jefferson district would drive by their neighborhood school to attend the new school.

The second option was to assign Sherwood children to the new school, which was their neighborhood school. This would ensure that all students had the shortest possible commute to school. The consequence of that action would be to create two elementary schools with sizable limited-English-speaking populations while leaving Jefferson untouched. This would also mean that there would be little cultural diversity at Jefferson.

The study group that I appointed worked diligently to develop a recommendation. One of the members was an engineer, and she generated a series of twenty different maps showing alternatives. After several long and contentious meetings, the group was split, with the majority favoring balancing the schools by English-language proficiency, while the minority advocated for neighborhood schools.

The pro-balance advocates were sincere people, and I can honestly say I believe that race was not a key issue influencing their decision. Rather, they believed that balancing the limited-English-speaking students among the three primary schools would create a better learning environment for all primary school children in Westborough. It was hard for me not to be moved by some of their comments.

- We have to finally bring the town together. We have to be proactive. The town can ill afford Jefferson Elementary's being perceived as better than the other schools.

- Sherwood Apartments is not even in a neighborhood. It is set off by itself across a major highway. The new school would not be Sherwood's neighborhood school as no student could walk there.

- Sherwood students will make Jefferson stronger as Jefferson students will be able to participate for the first time in multicultural education.

These arguments were compelling. One committee member had measured on her car odometer the extra mileage to transport Sherwood students to Jefferson instead of to the new school. She was very strong in her comments:

"Steve, the Sherwood children would have to travel a mile and a half longer to go to Jefferson. This would add approximately five minutes to their trip, which is not at all unreasonable. Is it worth continuing to split the community over an additional five minute bus drive for a small group of children?"

There is something about having people come at you with clear logic that compels you to think seriously about their position.

The opposition group, which wanted neighborhood schools, was also very persuasive with its arguments:

- You should not separate students on the basis of language alone.
- All students should be equally welcome in our schools.
- Every Westborough student comes together in the fourth grade in our large upper elementary school, so it is not imperative that schools be mixed at the primary level.

The advisory committee voted 7–4 to redistrict the schools in order to balance non-English-speaking students. As superintendent, I had the ultimate responsibility of making a recommendation to the school board concerning redistricting.

Make the Decision

President Eisenhower chose not to back the French, and Dien Bien Phu fell to the Vietminh. The president reasoned that the risk of intervention leading to a nuclear war with Russia and China was too great. He believed that in a war, due to America's superior nuclear arsenal, we would undoubtedly be successful militarily. He believed, however, that the United States would not benefit from a nuclear war as it would not serve America's purpose to watch as Russia and China were devastated, with millions of casualties and their lands destroyed. Eisenhower said no to military intervention in Vietnam and prevented a potential nuclear confrontation.

In Westborough, like Eisenhower, I went against the advice of many of my own advisors, and I recommended that the school board approve a neighborhood schools plan whereby no children were bused out of their neighborhoods. My rationale for the recommendation was that we had wonderful children in Westborough, and our schools were capable of educating all of them. To view minority students as a deficit to a school was repugnant to my personal philosophy. I did initiate a resource-allocation committee, which rebalanced the resources in the district in favor of Lincoln and the new school to meet their additional educational challenges. Additional teachers and supplies were assigned to Lincoln and the new school, which did somewhat calm parents' feelings as it demonstrated to them that the school system was concerned about equity in the three schools. Still, I do know that by this decision, I alienated a group of parents.

Results

The controversy over America's role in Vietnam did not end with the fall of the French legion at Dien Bien Phu. At the Geneva peace conference, Vietnam was split in two, with the Communists controlling the north, while the south became independent. President Eisenhower did commit large-scale economic aid to South Vietnam to try to keep that country from going Communist. This commitment eventually led to the beginnings of an American military presence under President John Kennedy and a huge military buildup and war under President Lyndon Johnson.

In my case, once the redistricting decision was made, the acrimony over the issue died down faster than I had anticipated. Providing additional resources to Lincoln and the new school did much to dispel the anger within the community over the decision. The school system also maintained lower student-teacher ratios at the two schools with minority membership, which was also appreciated by the parents. We superintendents sometimes make decisions based on a fine line between politics and education. There is a time when each approach is appropriate. My own guideline is that if no student will be disadvantaged by a decision, then politics can play a role. However, when children could be impacted negatively, I always try to do what is best educationally for the students. If I can look at myself in the mirror following my decision, I know in my heart it is right. Thomas Jefferson said it best: "In matters of style, swim with the current; in matters of principle, stand like a rock."

Reflection Points

- Do not be overwhelmed by the number and complexity of the problems brought to your attention. Certain decisions should be remanded to the staff member who is most appropriate to solve the problem. The superintendent should only deal with issues in which he has the primary authority or problems that cannot be resolved at other levels.

- Forming a committee to make a recommendation about an issue is an excellent strategy to resolve issues. It gets people involved and creates buy in. However, even with a committee, the superintendent should not abdicate his responsibility to do what he believes is ethically and morally correct.

- Important decisions should not be rushed as preparation and reflection are important to the process. Before making a decision, study extensively the background leading up to the problem. Solicit the ideas of people on all sides of the issue.

- There are seldom absolutely right and wrong answers to issues within the school system. Many of the issues that you confront as a superintendent are in the gray area. Review options and seek the best alternative.

- Make a decision compatible with your philosophy. Going off in different directions will show a lack of commitment and send mixed messages to staff and community. You have to live with your decisions, so make sure you are comfortable with them.

- Politics may be a factor in small decisions, such as whose phone calls are returned most quickly and how much time you are able to meet with certain people. However, decisions involving the welfare of children must be made on the basis of merit.
- Do not waffle or perseverate over decisions. Once you make a decision, move forward; don't look backward.

—⊂⊗⊃—

CHAPTER THREE

Vision

What a thrill to be appointed superintendent of schools in your district. Here you are at your first school board meeting, where you are the star. You try to appear modest as the school board chair extols your virtues, the press feverishly takes note of your statements, and the television cameras broadcast your smiling face into living rooms all over town. Suddenly, you are a celebrity as you are anointed the leader of the school system, and people look to you for direction. You have fulfilled your professional dream. How can it get any better than this? A simple answer is, it doesn't. Enjoy your brief time in the sun as the superintendency is a continuous uphill climb.

In Westborough, one of the first questions posed to me as a new superintendent by a member of the school board was, "What is your vision?" At that point I wasn't exactly sure what a vision was, but I knew I didn't have one, or at least one that I was aware of. I did not believe it was appropriate to tell them the absolute truth, that my vision was not to be fired, then unemployed, like several other former superintendents I knew. Instead, I tried something more conventional. "My vision is the achievement of excellence for every child in the Westborough Public Schools." Everyone smiled, but I knew that answer was superficial. After all, what did it mean? Who is against excellence? Does any superintendent actively advocate mediocrity? Vision was definitely an area in which I needed improvement. The problem was, I wasn't sure vision was important enough for me to devote time to. Yes, vision was now in vogue, but like former president George H. W. Bush, I questioned the importance of the "vision thing."

When I heard the term *vision*, I thought of Martin Luther King Jr. On a hot summer's day on August 28, 1963, King stood in front of a quarter of a million people in the shadow of the Lincoln Memorial describing his personal vision of an end to segregation and a new era of positive race relations for America:

> I have a dream that one day on the red hills of Georgia the sons of former slaves and the sons of former slave owners will be able to sit down together at the table of brotherhood. . . . And when this happens . . . we will be able to speed up that day when all God's children, black men and white men . . . will be able to join hands and sing in the words of the old Negro spiritual, "Free at last! Free at last! Thank God Almighty, we are free at last."

This personal vision articulated in Washington, D.C., by Dr. King also described in eloquent prose the collective vision of many Americans who believed in racial equality. Martin Luther King's words were more than a dream; they were a call to action. Based on that vision, he had been orchestrating a national movement for integration in the United States through nonviolent protest. His actions during the Montgomery bus boycott and the Birmingham sit-ins had already demonstrated his commitment to making his vision a reality for America. He was an inspirational leader who demonstrated fearlessness in standing up to police tactics of snarling dogs, high-pressure water hoses, and wooden clubs. Even when jailed in a Birmingham cell, his vision shone through as he used that time to compose *Letter from a Birmingham Jail*, in which he articulated the pressing need for civil rights for black Americans.

Martin Luther King would change the course of America. If that is what constitutes a successful vision, I didn't feel I was on the same radar screen. If setting a vision implied that I needed to do something as dramatic as confronting sadistic police and attack dogs, I would have forgone the vision approach altogether in favor of a safer approach.

Setting a vision does not imply historic changes, for if that were the case, there would be very few visions. I merely wanted to work with the staff and school board in setting a direction for education in Westborough that would benefit our students. I feared that without a plan, I might become a bureaucrat whose main concern was maintenance of the status quo and avoiding controversies. I did want to lead. The issue was, where did I want to lead?

As a new superintendent in the minds of the teachers and community, I was still a blank slate. What did I stand for? What was my vision? Even I was still not sure.

As a principal, I had never worried about a vision as the day-to-day hecticness of the job left little room for this type of reflection. As superintendent, I initially thought maybe I might borrow someone else's vision. Why reinvent the wheel? I reasoned. Improving education through technology was becoming a popular vision. However, this was not an area of strength for me. In fact, I probably had more crisis calls into the technology department than any other administrator. I was plagued by everything from frozen computer screens to jammed disks. Claiming technology as my vision might not be credible. How about, "Westborough is committed to educating the whole child"? That sounded even more pretentious. Was I assuming the teachers currently believed in educating part of the child and that I had to explain to them how to reach the rest of the student? I was looking for an idea to energize the community and faculty. It would have to be something that appealed to their hearts and minds. Amusing anecdotes and simplistic solutions just would not do it. A vision would have to be crafted to meet the needs of the district. As a model, I chose the approach of President John Kennedy.

Crafting a Personal Vision

In the 1960 presidential election, Democratic candidate John Fitzgerald Kennedy contested the Republican standard bearer, Vice President Richard Milhous Nixon. Critics assailed the forty-three-year-old Kennedy as too young and too inexperienced to become the nation's chief executive. John Kennedy attempted to turn the issue of his youth into an advantage by describing himself as the candidate of change. He referred to his vision as "The New Frontier." At first the details were vague, but as the campaign progressed, he provided more specifics. A vision doesn't have to be new; nor does it have to be presented in finished form. Rather, the vision must provide a look to the future, captivate people's imagination, and motivate them to buy in. Goals would have to be developed to show that the vision wasn't just a dream but a doable blueprint. Kennedy chose American idealism and self-sacrifice through service as a centerpiece of his new frontier.

John Kennedy's personal vision of service and self-sacrifice was molded from his own personal and family experiences. John Kennedy himself, in addition to serving in the U.S. House of Representatives and Senate, had served his nation heroically in war time. The story of his saving the crew members of PT-109 was in itself a testimony to his own personal courage and devotion to duty. Service had also been a trademark of the Kennedy family. His father, Joseph Kennedy, had served as ambassador to England, while his brother, Joe Junior, was a World War II navy pilot who lost his life attempting a heroic mission to knock out German V-2 rockets. In addition, his maternal grandfather, John "Honey Fitz" Fitzgerald, had served as mayor of Boston. When building a vision, personal experience is a helpful guide.

In constructing his own personal vision for the nation, Kennedy worked with talented young idealistic advisors, such as Theodore Schlesinger Jr., Kenneth O'Donnell, and Ted Sorenson, to refine his ideas. He also studied the way Franklin Roosevelt had energized the country and raised American morale by mobilizing three million young men for national service in the Civilian Conservation Corps during the Depression. Roosevelt had utilized these men aged eighteen to twenty-five living in rural camps to plant trees, build parks, stock rivers with fish, and work on other conservation projects. The program provided jobs to the unemployed and improved America's natural resources. Kennedy was to use the Roosevelt model well in molding his own ideas.

John Kennedy was not the only leader of the time to embrace the Roosevelt example of service by the young. Minnesota senator Hubert Humphrey, who had contested Kennedy for the Democratic nomination in 1960, had suggested a Peace Corps–type program during the campaign and had even filed legislation in Congress for such an institution. Several other congressional leaders also supported this type of initiative. However, Kennedy went one step further in developing the concept of youth service. While others had worked through the existing political establishment to attempt to develop a program, John Kennedy went directly to the young people to explain his vision of self-sacrifice and service to country. While other leaders went to great lengths to explain the logistics and rationale of such programs, Kennedy tapped into young people's emotions and their sense of idealism.

The message of building a better world through service first resonated from then presidential candidate Kennedy at a speech to faculty and students on October 14, 1960, at 2:00 a.m. on the steps of the Union at the University of Michigan. This unscheduled speech was Kennedy's response to the ten thousand students who showed up to greet the presidential candidate. They were not disappointed by the message. Kennedy made a clarion call for service:

> How many of you who are going to be doctors are willing to spend your days in Ghana? Technicians or engineers, how many of you are willing to work in the Foreign Service and spend your lives traveling around the world? On your willingness to that, not merely to spend one or two years in the service, but on your willingness to contribute part of your life to this country, I think, will depend the answer whether we as a free society can compete.

The response was overwhelming, with cheering and applause echoing through the campus. His vision had caught the imagination of the students. Hundreds of letters began to pour into candidate Kennedy's office saying that they would be willing to go to a foreign country and serve as American representatives. However, there were also skeptics. Richard Nixon referred to the proposed program as "a haven for draft dodgers," while President Eisenhower called it "the Kiddie Corps." Every leader has to be prepared to answer the critics, and Kennedy proved no exception.

I was certainly not thinking of anything nearly as grand as Kennedy's proposal. I merely needed a personal vision appropriate to the Westborough Public Schools and a suitable action plan to implement it. This did not sound that difficult as visions were now in vogue and springing up everywhere. Where should my vision come from? Certainly, it would have to come from my own beliefs based on my experiences. I sometimes am amazed at how little credit we superintendents give ourselves concerning our ability to articulate educational positions. After all, we usually have the experience of teaching in our own classrooms, administering schools and the school system, and completing coursework to be able to determine the most effective response to educational issues. A vision should describe where we intend to lead the district. The vision should be clear to teachers and parents and should be compelling enough to win their support. As I had previously served as an assistant superintendent in Westborough, I was aware of the issues in the district and felt comfortable determining a vision for the schools.

I narrowed my vision choice to three areas: community service, internationalism, and "active learning." In all three of these areas, I had considerable experience. I loved service learning, but we already had a strong program in place at the high school level. Although the topic certainly could be applied from kindergarten through twelfth grade, my concern was that the high school would continue to be the key player with a smaller emphasis in kindergarten through eighth grade. I decided that Westborough could easily just continue in this direction without committing to that as a vision. I was also looking for something broader. I had similar concerns about internationalism. Certainly, we had elements of understanding different cultures in the curriculum at all levels, and internationalism was certainly important. Still, it was the high school that was the leader in this area. Again, I was looking for something that could more easily be adopted from kindergarten through twelfth grade. I was also looking for a broad vision that could eventually encompass both service learning and internationalism. Active learning appeared to satisfy these criteria.

As a principal, I had observed many classes. The teachers who appeared most successful were the ones who got the students actively involved in their learning. Those classes were vibrant and alive in contrast to the passive classrooms where students were most often lectured to or drilled. To my mind as a high school teacher, my students were most often motivated through debates, projects, simulations, reports, and, my own personal favorite, the research paper. If I was going to lead a school system, I wanted to lead in the direction of students' active involvement in their own learning. Certainly, in time, service learning and internationalism could be part of a plan to implement this vision.

The vision that I articulated in Westborough was to develop a community of active learners who would demonstrate their learning gains through improved classroom performance. I wanted to see the students become significantly involved in their own learning. This all sounded exciting, but I would have to describe to people what this would look like. A vision is only a vision if it pictures a place to which we are going. When I described active learning to the community, I talked of classroom instructional strategies that emphasized projects, problem solving, experimentation, writing, cooperative learning, and other active-learning experiences. When I visited a classroom, I wanted to see students engaged in their learning and excited about it. This did not discount the value of memorizing important topics, such as the multiplication tables, or listening to lectures on important topics. What active learning meant was that the teachers engaged the learners and made them part of the process.

Still, where would we start on such a large initiative? Westborough was a high-achieving system. Why would people embrace a change in methodology? One thing my experience taught me was that the number-one reason that teachers change behavior is that they think the change will be good for students. This emphasis on active learning fortunately also coincided with some major changes that were happening in our district in certain classrooms.

Many of our teachers in the elementary school had been attending language arts workshops that emphasized the need for more realistic, action-oriented classroom-learning activities for students, such as reading authentic literature, participating in literary discussion groups, and process writing. This contrasted with our current language arts approach of basal readers with their dull stories accompanied by workbooks that emphasized drill and practice. As I knew that all the academic disciplines could not be changed at once, I would support this movement and focus on redesigning the language arts curriculum as a good place to start to implement the vision.

The initial plan for implementing the vision would be simple: In all primary language arts classrooms, students would read high-interest authentic literature rather than basal selections, which tended to be dull and contrived. Through this authentic literature, the teachers would stress comprehension, fluency, and phonics. The emphasis would be on students' gaining understanding of literature by being actively engaged in their reading. Comprehension would take on a new importance.

Process writing would be emphasized at all grade levels with writing folders compiled in each grade, which would move forward with the student as the student progressed through the grades. Students would be trained as active young writers with minimal emphasis on workbooks.

Writing across the curriculum would be emphasized in all academic disciplines in kindergarten through grade twelve, as writing would be used as a vehicle to stimulate ideas in students.

I was comfortable with the approach of targeting language arts as the first initiative to implement the vision as I had once taught English and had been active as a principal in all aspects of the English program. Still, I had taught and administered at the high school level many years before. In addition, I was not knowledgeable about how the language arts were best taught in the elementary schools. I would now be calling for a major revision of the existing language arts curriculum and instructional practices, as well as advocating for extensive expenditures for books and for teacher training. Westborough was already a high-performing district, and I knew that there would be people who would say, "If it is not broken, why fix it?" I was concerned about failure. After all, what would happen if the program proved to be unsuccessful and our students did worse than we did in previous years?

Before I articulated this vision, I continually gauged teacher reaction. I authorized many out-of-district workshops for literature-based reading and process writing, and the response of the participating teachers was usually positive. I could feel that this was a beginning of a surge of momentum for change.

Like President Kennedy, I also had skeptics. I held open meetings with the community and had a very mixed reaction. Although some parents praised my desire to motivate young readers and writers, other people were negative. My favorite critic was a mother who, following my presentation at a parent-teacher organization meeting, spoke up and stated, "This method makes no sense. I am the queen of phonics and believe pure phonics is the only way to educate children to read and write." Sometimes, the hardest part of the job is not laughing at the absurd. I was not aware that royalty had resided in Westborough. I attempted to explain to her that the teachers would continue to use phonics, but these skills would be integrated into authentic student reading and writing instead of being used in isolation as was then the practice. I emphasized that we would still use phonics as a main component of our reading program, but we would also increase our emphasis on comprehension and fluency. The "queen of phonics" was not convinced, and other nay-sayers joined her in criticizing the proposed program. An emotional parent cautioned me to beware of adopting untried new educational theories. "Remember the New Math," she warned with the same fervor with which Texans once shouted, "Remember the Alamo."

Even among the faculty, there was a degree of negativism as some people felt we were moving too quickly in an unproven direction. However, like President Kennedy, I knew I needed to set a new direction, and despite the opposition, this activity-oriented constructivist approach in language arts made sense. Now, how was I to get the commitment from the staff to move Westborough in this direction?

Setting the Collective Vision

Following his election, John Kennedy planned to state to the nation his vision in his inaugural address. Most people already viewed him as a dynamic statesman, and there was high expectation that his first speech as president would be compelling. From Kennedy's point of view, here was his chance to capture the imagination of the American people and gain their support. This was the opportunity to propel the United States to a "new frontier" and, in doing so, to separate his administration from the more conservative thinking of the Eisenhower administration.

Inauguration day was frigid, with temperatures dipping below freezing. However, this worked to Kennedy's advantage as he looked dynamic with his healthy tan and thick crop of brown hair. He stood for hours in the cold without a hat or topcoat. The country and the world could see the vitality of this youthful president. This contrasted with the outgoing President Eisenhower, who at age seventy appeared tired from an eight-year administration during which he had survived a major heart attack. John Kennedy looked prepared for the challenge of the nation's highest office. The president was ready to move, and it appeared the country was ready to move with him.

Kennedy's inaugural address was a commitment to idealism, optimism, and service. The ring of his vision could be heard in the words

> To those people in the huts and villages across the globe struggling to break the bonds of mass misery, we pledge our best efforts to help them help themselves, for whatever period is required, not because the Communists may be doing it, not because we seek their votes, but because it is right. If a free society cannot help the many who are poor, it cannot save the few who are rich.

Later in his speech, John Kennedy further implored Americans, "Ask not what your country can do for you—ask what you can do for your country."

His vision was clear, and there was overwhelming support for the new president. Newspapers across the country praised the speech as setting a clear direction. The vision was now set, and Kennedy, to be successful, would have to deliver on his pledge.

I did not aspire to worldwide recognition, so my task was considerably easier. I had to instill a common vision in Westborough teachers to create classrooms that were interactive and activity oriented. As Kennedy emphasized the Peace Corps as the first component of his program, I emphasized the development of a new curriculum for language arts as a first step in revitalizing the entire curriculum.

Here was I without any formal background in reading instruction, giving direction to people who had taught reading and writing in their classrooms, some for over thirty years. I would have to clarify what the expectation was for them and why change was imperative. Fortunately, many highly regarded teachers were already moving in this direction. I wanted everyone to hear the same message so they could understand the components of this active language arts approach.

To convey this new direction, I instituted workshops in all schools led by an area consultant who had previously impressed the teachers and me during a full day workshop she had conducted at a nearby college. What impressed me most about her was her nonthreatening manner and the passion with which she delivered her message. She was able to articulate concretely what I believed but did not have the background to articulate. She impressed the staff as knowledgeable and, with her years of experience as a primary school teacher, very credible. I contracted with her to work in all of the Westborough schools not only to explain the theory but to demonstrate how to implement it. In the elementary schools, she actually took over classes for a period of time to model the reading-writing connection and what she referred to as "readers' workshop" and "writers' workshop." Seeing the process in action made people much more accepting as they saw their students respond well to her instruction. She was also very patient with teachers reluctant to change their existing strategies. This consultant provided not only instruction but support. The number of converts began to increase, and a critical mass of teachers appeared to be moving now in favor of the new approach.

Resources were put into place to continue support for this initiative. People who wanted to visit other schools before making a commitment were allowed to do so. Additional speakers at all grade levels were brought in. We even had staff-development dinner meetings that drew over one hundred teachers and administrators. Our director of food services would prepare lasagna dinners before each session. That in itself helped raise morale as I heard more than one teacher say, "At least I don't have to make dinner for the family tonight." More importantly, teachers talking to teachers about language arts strategies, even before the start of the sessions, stimulated thinking and new ideas. This approach energized the staff and made the changes appear more teacher friendly as the people who attended these sessions served as support groups for each other. An excitement was being created. The conversation was no longer about change dictated by the administration. The discussion was now about what was the best method to educate children. The vision was now no longer mine or some small group of teachers'; rather, it was becoming internalized by the teachers in the school system.

Of course, as in many systems, the most difficult group to get to accept change was the high school teachers. High school teachers often portray any attempt at change brought in from the outside as a "lowering of standards." At one meeting of high school teachers, I encouraged them to attend a three-day program called "Writing to Learn," which was being presented at Bard College in upstate New York. This initiative interfaced wonderfully with the interdisciplinary approach that we were implementing in kindergarten through grade eight. One of the teachers in the room said with a smile, "If you are truly committed to this approach, if we go, will you go with us?" I couldn't figure why they would even want me. High school teachers do not usually reach out to the administration, so I could not discern whether this was a challenge or a sincere request. After a long week with my night meetings, a four-hour ride each way and a three-day workshop with teachers would not be my ideal way to spend a long weekend. There was no way I wanted to take this type of challenge.

On Friday morning of the next week, two English teachers, a history teacher, a science teacher, and I set out in a van for Bard College. I looked at it this way: there were plenty of family events that I dreaded attending, and some of them turned out to be very enjoyable. Maybe the workshop would not be that bad after all. To the teachers, it was an opportunity to take advantage of a staff-development opportunity in new surroundings. To me it was a chance to gain converts. During that institute, we worked as a team in each session. During the conference, I got to know the teachers and heard their concerns about time limitations in the curriculum, which were legitimate. With all the other learning activities they did each day, they were concerned there would not be time for this initiative. Although their buy-in was tempered, two teachers did conduct workshops in writing across the curriculum at the high school when they returned. They proved very influential in getting other teachers to adopt the program in their classrooms. Equally importantly, my participation demonstrated to the high school faculty my commitment to the process of active learning.

There was another key constituency that needed to support the vision, and that was the public. The school board was an unexpectedly easy sell. They knew the teachers who were doing the intergrade activity-oriented language arts approach, and they referred to these teachers as "the good teachers," as compared to the "bad teachers," whom they perceived as boring the students. Although this was a major simplification of the issue, the credibility of the teachers who stepped forward to advance the program sold the program. The budget priority was the acquisition of thousands of small paperback books, which would become the foundation for the literature-based reading program. The school board was surprisingly supportive, and funding for other programs was postponed for a year in order to provide the resources for the new language arts approach. As the school board meetings were televised, the parents could see the school board's support and hear the reasons for it. Most parents eventually came on board, although there were still concerns. There was some skepticism that we were trying to sneak in "whole language" and eliminate phonics instruction, which was not true. Unlike whole language, this approach would include a strong, definable, phonics component, as well as a built-in accountability model. To alleviate parent fears, we ran literary nights and brought in speakers. However, the real sell again appeared to be that the "good teachers" liked it. There was also a certain excitement about anything new, and people are drawn to the enthusiasm and excitement. The vision appeared to be winning converts. Now, the remaining question was, With many people now in agreement, could we deliver?

Implementation

Less than two months after his inauguration, President Kennedy, by executive order, set up the Peace Corps. To lead the corps, Kennedy appointed Sargent Shriver, who was married to his sister Eunice. Shriver proved to be an outstanding appointment. He had proved his value to Kennedy as a very effective political organizer during the presidential election. Shriver was efficient, very outgoing, and, like Kennedy, very optimistic. Optimism is a crucial ingredient for winning supporters. Shriver would build a talented team of idealistic assistants to launch the start of the Peace Corps, including high-profile Olympic decathlon gold medalist Rafer Johnson. Shriver designed the program that John Kennedy had pledged to the American people.

Applications rolled in rapidly. President Kennedy in his speeches referred to these young people as his "ambassadors of peace." Kennedy made it clear that the goals of the Peace Corps would not be political. The mission was for Americans to help create a better world. Peace Corps workers would not be paid but would receive a small stipend for subsistence. Their commitment was for two years, during which time they would travel to developing countries and live and work with the native people to improve conditions in the host country. Kennedy stated that the Peace Corps exemplified American idealism. Service to the underprivileged was a priority for his administration. No more would the world see the image of the ugly American who merely wanted to exploit the resources of Third World nations. Instead, they would see our idealistic young people at work, side by side with the local population, helping people to help themselves. America was now on the moral high ground, and Third World people often liked what they saw. Our image now was of being helpful rather than selfish and arrogant. People began to know Americans and like Americans, which served as a counterweight to the Russian propaganda portraying residents of the United States as greedy and uncaring.

The applications continued to increase as Kennedy energized a generation of young people who had never before considered engaging in government. Peace Corps workers served as teachers, health-care workers, small-business advisors, agricultural agents, technicians, and construction workers. Due to the efforts of these American volunteers, schools, roads, public buildings, and hospitals were constructed, and farming was improved. Underdeveloped nations were seeing America at its best. Kennedy's vision had become America's vision, with the American public overwhelmingly approving the program.

As President Kennedy needed Sargent Shriver, I needed energetic, committed leadership to implement the vision. Support of the principals and other administrators would not be enough. The program needed a cadre of trained people who were dedicated to this process. I selected three longtime, well-respected members of the Westborough faculty as the coordinating group, and I gave them time to meet during school and after school to refine the direction of the program.

The coordinating committee was assisted by curriculum writers in each school who, during the summer, would develop the curriculum for each grade. Over twenty-five Westborough teachers served as paid curriculum writers. Support was also provided to all language arts teachers. Money for staff-development projects and summer curriculum writing was directed toward language arts. If people wanted to go to a conference or to visit another school, the answer was yes. There may have been no money for other subject areas, but language arts money was available. We also continued to bring in staff developers to speak in our district and to present model lessons. These people would shore up reluctant teachers and demonstrate how a literature-based program, accompanied by a process-writing approach, could succeed. The critical mass was growing stronger. We did move forward at a rapid rate, but there was also some resentment. Principals had to work continually to encourage reluctant teachers.

A second component of implementation was placing a full-time curriculum-resource teacher in each elementary school to ensure that assistance would be available as needed. The high school and middle schools already had department chairs to provide curriculum and instructional leadership, and secondary teachers had more time available during the day for preparation. At the elementary school level, these curriculum resource people, in addition to providing support, would work with teachers to ensure that the curriculum was implemented uniformly in all Westborough elementary classrooms. These people modeled lessons, secured resources, team-taught with the teachers, answered questions, and were available every day to make certain assistance was available when needed.

Finally, the last step was removing basal readers from all classrooms. The basals were the old textbooks with manufactured stories drawn from phonics sounds. It was the method of the past and not the future. When this was done, you would have thought we had removed oxygen from the system. There was a huge outcry from a group of teachers who felt most comfortable with these books. Although it was their recommendation, the principals and the coordinating committee made sure the teachers knew that I was the one responsible for this action. As superintendent, the buck stops with you. The basals were soon extinct. Westborough was on its way following a new plan. There was no turning back unless the results warranted reconsideration.

Results

The true measure of a program is whether it meets the goal for which it is designed. John Kennedy judged the Peace Corps a success based on the number of requests for volunteers by foreign governments world-wide, who were impressed by the work of Peace Corps workers in improving living conditions. Since 1961, presidents from both parties have supported the Peace Corps, and to date over one hundred fifty thousand Americans have served as volunteers. Peace Corps members have visited over one hundred foreign countries. Kennedy's vision of idealism and service is exemplified in the Peace Corps today.

The active-learning language arts curriculum is still used in classrooms in Westborough today. Teachers use real literature to develop student reading skills and combine it with the process-writing approach. Reading comprehension and writing skills have improved, although spelling scores have declined. Teachers also assert that the program has created more motivated students, whom they believe will be lifelong readers. I view this perception of success as the stimulus to keep the program going. Over a number of years, active-learning curricula were instituted for math, science, and history.

Overall, active learning is still the priority in the school system. The level of commitment to active learning varies among teachers. Many are philosophically committed to this approach, a significant number comply because it is the way the district curricula are written and because it is the method encouraged by the principals, and a very small number conform but would prefer a more traditional approach. Still, classrooms in the system are active, which motivates students to become independent learners.

Reflection Points

- A personal vision will allow you to set a clear direction. However, you must endeavor to develop a collective vision to make change happen. In developing a collective vision, speak with staff and parents to gain a greater understanding of their perceptions of the needs of the system.
- Make your vision simple to understand. You should be able to articulate a vision in two minutes or less.
- Vision should tap into the emotions of people and get them excited. Vision should allow a look into the future of the school system and serve as a guiding force.

- A commitment to a vision binds a school system together. For the process to be successful, the staff has to believe that the direction in which the system is moving is good for children.

- Show your personal commitment to the vision. Visit classrooms to let teachers know that the vision is important enough for you to observe classroom instruction. Provide staff development to ensure that there is a common understanding of the vision and what is needed for its implementation. Provide the necessary resources to implement the vision.

- Work with principals to set time lines for implementation of goals consistent with the vision at each school. Although there will be differences in activities between classrooms and between schools, the goals should be the same.

- Vision implies a change in the status quo, and this will cause discomfort. The principal must work with those who do not initially endorse the changes.

- Remain positive and optimistic, even when there are setbacks and opposition.

CHAPTER FOUR

—⚬⚬⚬—

Risk Taking

The willingness to take a risk is an important ingredient for success as a superintendent. Risk taking also causes superintendents anxiety and sleepless nights. Implicit in risk is an uncertain outcome, and unexpected results can prove disastrous to our reputations and careers. Most school boards do support their superintendents' being risk takers. However, when risks prove unsuccessful, we as superintendents often stand alone. An old maxim states, Success has one hundred fathers while failure is an orphan. This well describes the stakes involved in taking a chance.

Mr. Miyaki in the film *The Karate Kid* accurately explains the rationale for risk taking. When his teenage protégé Daniel jokes about confronting the karate teacher of the teens who are continually harassing him, Mr. Miyaki gives him a realistic perspective:

> Daniel: "I'll just go straight to the school and straighten it out with the teacher."
> Mr. Miyaki: "Now using [your] head."
> Daniel: "I was only kidding."
> Mr. Miyaki: "Why kidding?"
> Daniel: "I'll get killed if I show up there."
> Mr. Miyaki: "[You will] get killed anyway."

This dialogue describes the plight of a leader. Bold action is accompanied by high risk and consequences. However, inaction does not guarantee safety as it may only make you appear weak, indecisive, and easily intimidated. A superintendent whose character is suspect in the community cannot be an effective leader.

Leaders in all fields confront the potential of failure and disappointment when they take a chance. However, what makes our risks more problematic is the public nature of our jobs. In Westborough, the cable station televises the biweekly school board meetings, and the meetings are rebroadcast continually throughout the next week. I'm surprised at how many people in Westborough have told me that they regularly view these proceedings. I attend all the school board meetings and know how boring they can be. I am surprised anyone would become a regular viewer without financial compensation. Local newspapers also feature our decisions, so those people who are unable to watch the school board meetings live or taped can learn about the meeting from the perspective of the reporter. When you take a risk, and it is not successful, you are suddenly front-page news. However, the general public is not the only group to review difficult decisions. Teachers, athletic and music boosters, parents of special education children, and many other special interest groups also monitor your actions. What appears a wise decision to one group may appear foolhardy to others.

Recently, I attended a conference where the speaker said that school leaders should be risk takers like Christopher Columbus. He emphasized that if Columbus did not have the courage to sail west, then America might not have been founded until years later. Comparing us to Columbus is not relevant. Let's leave aside the issue of Columbus's alleged participation in the genocide of Native Americans, which is horrific enough; Columbus's management techniques were, at best, suspect. On his first voyage, he kept two sets of books. The set for his personal review was accurate while the other set was fabricated so the crew would think they were closer to home than they actually were. If a superintendent kept two sets of books, an auditor would charge him with financial malfeasance. Columbus also may have faced the Atlantic voyage with only three relatively small boats and a potentially mutinous crew, but he was still the fleet commander far from review by King Ferdinand and Queen Isabella of Spain. We, as public officials, are seldom alone as we face the daily scrutiny of school board, public, and news media. Such public exposure and potential for criticism often inhibit school leaders from taking risks. For a school leader, risk has to be tempered by judgment. A superintendent has to manage risk in the same way as an insurance company. In their advertisement, Prudential urges you to own a piece of the rock. However, if you have a history of poor health, you cannot secure a share of anything with Prudential. Companies will not invest in an enterprise that does not project a reasonable return. It is the same with risk management for superintendents. Risks can pay huge dividends for students and the community if they are successful. However, speculation can result in failure and a charge of recklessness. In taking a risk, superintendents must first measure the potential benefit for the children in the school system and weigh that against the resources needed and the potential for failure.

There will be times, even after only a cursory review, that you believe a risk is well worth taking. For example, when I met with a neighboring superintendent, he proposed that Westborough join with his and forty other districts worldwide to create a virtual high school. Each of the participating districts would have one of its instructors teach a course on the internet, which would be available to students at any of the forty participating schools. Westborough students could then enroll in any of these courses. This was a risk in the sense that we would have to commit money for teacher salaries, training, and startup fees for a program that was untested. Still, it appeared worth taking the chance as it would open up new courses and provide a different perspective to Westborough students. This futuristic idea was worth a strong commitment of funds and support and proved successful as over eighty Westborough students annually enroll in the virtual high school.

Conversely, sometimes you judge that the time is not right for a risk as the dangers outweigh potential benefits. The Westborough High School principal showed me a plan whereby we would expand the career-education program by partnering with the Chamber of Commerce to place students into internships in businesses throughout the Westborough area. I liked the idea of this type of project expansion. Still, the commitment to hire several career-education teachers, at a time when we were going through difficult financial conditions, I viewed as a mistake. Due to the timing, I did not support this initiative. Even though I did not take advantage of an opportunity to create a program to help students, I still feel my judgment was sound. Being a risk taker does not mean jumping at every promising opportunity. Rather, it means making judgments as to the best approach for the school system at the time.

One dangerous approach to successful leadership is waffling on risky issues. This type of behavior will lead to questions about your commitment. This dilemma happened to me on a major decision about administration. In Westborough during the planning phase for a new intermediate school, our new principal recommended hiring two assistants to help her administer a school of nine hundred students. The plan was to have a "school within a school" model. Instead of one large school, there would be three small schools, with populations drawn equally from grades four, five, and six, each with its own administrator and guidance counselor. Through this approach, students would feel like part of a small school of three hundred rather than one of nine hundred in a large school. I supported the plan enthusiastically, although it was a calculated risk due to the high level of administrative staffing. Because of the school board's openness to the idea and my strong support, the school board approved the proposal 5–0. I publicly advocated for the administrative staffing in the community over a three-month period that preceded town meeting; in many Massachusetts towns, town meeting is where voters assemble to appropriate money for all town spending. It is the time that the superintendent makes his final case for the school budget, and town meeting members can approve, lower, or raise that budget figure.

The community response to my proposal was very negative as people felt that an elementary school, even with nine hundred students, did not require two assistants. Due to the fierce opposition and my fear of imminent defeat, I withdrew the proposal immediately before town meeting.

My decision to retreat hurt my credibility with the school board. As the school board had backed my decision, they felt deceived by my change of position. They also had endured a lot of criticism because they believed in the idea, and they had shown faith in me. To make matters worse, I disappointed many parents who believed the plan made sense educationally. My decision to pull back at the last minute made me look to the public like a person more interested in saving his reputation than in serving the best interests of children. It also sent a message to the community that you could intimidate the superintendent by exerting pressure. I felt like a baseball hitter who had already broken his wrist on a swing but did not follow through and try to hit the ball. I vowed to myself that the next time I would do it correctly. That time would come quickly. The major risk would concern ability grouping. This would prove to be a contentious issue within our school system as it meant a total change in classroom structure. This decision was analogous to the risk that President Johnson took when he worked to put through the Civil Rights Bill of 1964, which radically changed the social structure of America.

Philosophy Check

Risky decisions and actions must align with a leader's personal philosophy. How can a superintendent convince others of the need for action unless he himself is philosophically committed? Leadership means that you stand for something. This was the plight of President Lyndon Johnson. As a Southern congressman and senator, he had not been a civil rights advocate. However, after becoming president following the assassination of President John Kennedy, he made a huge philosophical shift.

Johnson was never a hard-core racist like some Southern politicians. This may be partially attributable to the fact that he had grown up in the economically poor hill country of West Central Texas, where race was not a hot-button issue as the region had very few black families. Lyndon Johnson had also taught for one year in a segregated school where he taught fourth grade to an all Mexican American class in Cotulla, Texas. The teaching experience influenced Johnson's views on race. In 1935, Lyndon Johnson was appointed director of the National Youth Administration in Texas. Here again, Johnson showed an ability to reach beyond race. He gained a reputation with blacks as a fair man as he took a genuine interest in projects of benefit to blacks, such as construction of new buildings on the campuses of black colleges. Lyndon Johnson was not a typical Southern politician of the age. Although he still maintained a traditional Southern attitude about the need for a separation of the races, he did quietly demonstrate concern for minorities. Still, his risks were minor. None of the issues he pursued was considered very controversial at the time. Even when elected to the House of Representatives in 1936, Johnson continued his "moderate Southern views" on race.

When Lyndon Johnson campaigned for the Senate in 1948, his attitude became significantly more conservative politically. Race was a big issue statewide in Texas, and many voters would only support candidates who would continue the tradition of white supremacy. During his first senatorial campaign, Johnson stressed to his constituency that he would not support civil rights or any form of racial equality.

Following his election victory, Lyndon Johnson quickly allied himself with the powerful conservative Southern leadership in the senate. Southerners dominated the senate through longevity, which allowed them to hold powerful committee chairmanships. Johnson particularly attached himself to Senator Richard Russell, a segregationist, who was chair of the powerful Senate Armed Services Committee. Johnson's loyalty was repaid when Russell appointed Johnson to his committee. In 1955, with the support of Senator Russell and other powerful Southern leaders, Lyndon Johnson was elected Democratic majority leader. Johnson was, at that time, still a reliable foe of civil rights legislation.

As his power in the Senate grew, he was willing to take some amount of risk. He did actively support passage of the civil rights act of 1957, which expanded the federal role in protecting the rights of blacks. Johnson saw the bill as a compromise, and he made sure the bill did not contain provisions that would be anathema to the South. He convinced his Southern colleagues to go along with the bill rather than fighting it by telling them that this bill would quiet the blacks and their liberal allies, while allowing a " business as usual situation" to continue. He emphasized to his supporters that this bill could be a lot worse if the liberals had their way. The bill passed, and Johnson skillfully prevented the Democratic Party from splitting along regional lines on this issue. His support of the bill was a small risk that paid large dividends for him politically as he became viewed as a man of national stature rather than just a regional politician. Little did Johnson realize that just a few years later he would face a real risk when the death of President John

Kennedy catapulted him to the presidency. He then had to confront the emotional issue of civil rights.

The biggest risk I had to take as superintendent was the confronting issue of ability grouping at the elementary and middle school levels. This was a volatile topic in the community as many parents of high-ability students supported our traditional program of homogenous grouping (by ability) for instruction. In ability grouping, the top students were all placed in the same classroom, while the students who had the most difficulty were put into separate classrooms. The parents of students who demonstrated lower achievement were now advocating a change to heterogeneous grouping (mixing of students of different abilities in the same classroom).

Like Lyndon Johnson, I was brought up in a traditional system. I had been a high school teacher and principal in high schools where grouping was the norm. I had taught Advanced Placement U.S. history and enjoyed the experience of having the academically talented students together in one class. I looked forward to that class each day as these students were frequently able to analyze historical issues effortlessly. Many of these students would later go on to attend Ivy League colleges, and I confess that I felt like a scholar in front of them as I led high-level discussions on historical concepts and events. I also enjoyed the lower-achieving groups but for different reasons. I liked the way they related to me on a personal basis rather than on a strictly academic basis. I was more relaxed with these groups as they were not nearly as competitive with each other, which contributed to a more relaxed learning environment. When I became a high school principal, I unquestionably believed in ability grouping. However, I became disturbed by the elitism that was so prevalent in my high school. One day, a student approached me and asked if I knew the meaning of the acronym CAP, which was the name of our alternative school. When I told him I didn't know, he told me CAP stood for "Certified Animal Person."

It was disheartening to hear students put down other students with lesser academic ability. I had never thought at all about the impact of grouping at elementary and middle schools, for if it was effective for the high school, why wouldn't it be effective at the lower levels? Like Lyndon Johnson, the death of my boss, the former superintendent, propelled me to the next level. Also, like Lyndon Johnson, I would face the challenge of deeply divisive differences of opinion within the public.

Decision Time

Before taking a risk, a leader must assess the potential benefits. Lyndon Johnson could see very clearly that segregation was a backward looking approach to race relations. The Civil War had ended slavery almost one hundred years before, but Jim Crow segregation laws still kept Southern blacks in an inferior social, political, and economic position. Johnson observed how even former president Eisenhower, who had never been a civil rights advocate, had sent the 101st Airborne Division to Little Rock, Arkansas, in 1956 to protect black teenagers who were integrating Little Rock Central High School. Lyndon Johnson had supported Eisenhower's decision to send troops to stop the violence.

Later, as vice president, Lyndon Johnson, with all Americans, could witness the scenes on television of the mob violence directed against black protesters in Birmingham, Alabama, and other Southern cities in response to demonstrations for civil rights. Lyndon Johnson could also clearly see the blacks winning over the hearts and minds of many people all over the world through nonviolent protest. Black students were using sit-ins at lunch counters to protest segregated facilities and having these demonstrations disrupted by Southern sheriffs who frequently carted the students off to jail. Americans could also witness the success of the March on Washington in the summer of 1963, where Martin Luther King spoke not only to the two hundred thousand participants but to the nation and the world. John Kennedy, as president, had spoken out for a need for a civil rights bill. With President Kennedy's death, Lyndon Johnson, as the country's chief executive, would now confront the same issue.

President Johnson believed the South had to change. People all over the world were seeing Southerners as haters and "rednecks." Johnson also identified with the struggles of the poor. Although he was far from a liberal on the issue of race, he came to believe segregation was morally wrong. He knew that segregation was isolating the South as it separated the region morally and politically from the rest of the country. In addition, Southerners were increasingly viewed as pariahs, and many large companies chose to invest in more progressive regions.

Lyndon Johnson also saw that segregation could hurt the Democratic Party and was politically a detriment to him as president. John

Kennedy had been elected president in 1960 by winning more than 70 percent of the black vote. Supporting civil rights was an opportunity for President Johnson to demonstrate to the blacks that the Democrats, long associated with Southern segregation, were open to their issues. However, this strategy was high risk for the Democrats, for just as a civil rights bill would increase black support for the party, it would decrease white votes for the Democrats in the South and possibly bequeath political power in the Southern states to the Republican Party.

Politically, integration was also a high risk for Johnson himself. His career was on the line as many people would judge his leadership based on this issue. Johnson could no longer straddle the civil rights issue as he did in the late 1950s. Either he was going with the new direction of the country or he would merely maintain the old order. Johnson would later recount to historian Doris Kearns Goodwin,

> I knew . . . that if I didn't get out in front of this issue, they [the liberals] would get me. They'd throw up my background against me, they'd use it to prove that I was incapable of bringing unity to the land I loved so much. . . . I couldn't let that happen. I had to produce a civil rights bill that was even stronger than the one they'd have gotten if Kennedy had lived. Without this, I'd be dead before I could even begin.

Johnson, with all his heart, soul, and political instinct, decided to take a risk. He would stake his presidency and his own legacy on this issue.

My risk, early in my central office career, was also in the area of equality. I was becoming increasingly concerned about the effect of ability grouping at the elementary and middle school levels. The latest books and articles were coming out in favor of mixed grouping rather than ability grouping in elementary school and middle school. The message was consistent: ability grouping held back certain students, isolated them, and made them feel inadequate. The Harvard Education Review, the Association for Supervision and Curriculum Development, and Phi Delta Kappa were all publishing articles favorable to mixed-ability grouping. Ann Wheelock, a professor from the University of California, Los Angeles, had just written a book advocating mixed grouping, which was being widely discussed at professional conferences. Aside from the other issues associated with grouping, segregating children on a perception of ability just sounded un-American. It became increasingly difficult to justify sorting students at an early age rather than giving them an opportunity to succeed.

When I visited our primary schools, one activity which demonstrated to me the unfairness of ability grouping was "round-robin reading." During this process, each student would read aloud individually while the rest of the class listened. Students in the top reading groups would literally fly through the books, with each student reading a portion. It was a delight to witness the fluency and the enthusiasm of the children. However, round-robin reading in the low reading groups just didn't look right to me. As I sat there observing, each reader would slowly and painfully sound out every syllable of the most difficult words in the story. By the time the story ended, I was looking at twenty bored young people. While listening, I could often feel myself suppressing a yawn. The strategies in the top classes often appeared stimulating, with an emphasis on projects and creative thought. In the lower-achieving classes, drill sheets and workbook pages were far more abundant. There had to be another way.

Still, this was a difficult issue. The teachers were divided on the topic. A significantly large group of teachers supported heterogeneous grouping as they believed it was most compatible with our new direction of active learning. Others believed that if they did not sort the students into different classrooms, the top students would be bored while the bottom group would be lost. In a meeting with the teachers, a second-grade teacher said, "Believe me, ability grouping makes sense. We do make provisions to motivate the little ones [students of lower ability]." I disliked the term the *little ones* as it sounded like these children were genetic mutants. Still the dialogue was a good one, and I believe all teachers, in their own way, wanted to do what they perceived as the best for students.

Among parents, the issue was extremely controversial. Parents of high-performing students tended to favor ability grouping out of fear that mixing students together would slow their child's progress. Parents of lower-ability students tended to want to see the classes mixed so that their children would have better reading role models. I also saw in these parents of lower achievers a tremendous desire to correct what they considered a major problem. I had seen a similar look in 1974 when special education was just beginning, and parents were demanding more support for their children. Whether parents are fighting for special education services or fighting to break down the segregation of ability grouping, they are a formidable force. I knew which side would eventually win this debate, and I could feel the tide turning. I also became increasingly sensitive to the self-concept of students. When I visited classes at different grade levels, I could see a change in the attitude of students. In kindergarten, students all believed that they were smart, and they demonstrated confidence in class. However, as students in so-called low groups progressed through the grades, separated from their higher-achieving classmates, increasingly they changed their perception. They began to believe that they were not very smart, and they attributed their failings to lack of intelligence. Once this happened, effort declined, and so did performance. With this realization, I had turned a corner in my own career and was willing to take the risk by challenging the traditional approach of grouping by ability. I believed education could make a difference for all children and that our mission should be to offer stimulating challenges for all students.

Moving Forward

President Johnson was strong-minded. He decided the nation would have a civil rights bill, and it would be so strong that it would break down the barriers of legal segregation. Unlike former president John Kennedy, he felt no need to compromise. Kennedy was a Massachusetts liberal who would have been confronting the Southern establishment with civil rights, so he would have probably been somewhat flexible in his approach. Johnson, on the other hand, was part of the Southern establishment. He believed, although he was now at odds with the other Southerners, that he had the ability and the credibility to bring strong legislation forward.

Southern politicians felt betrayed by Lyndon Johnson's conversion and his unwillingness to support a compromise. Former colleagues in the Senate, including his former mentor, Senator Richard Russell, came to regard him as a turncoat and a traitor to his region.

With his breaking of personal ties to the Southern establishment, Johnson had found a new set of allies, advocates for civil rights. He had his vice president, Hubert Humphrey, a well-known Northern liberal crusader for civil rights, become the floor manager for the bill. With his strong ties to liberal causes, Humphrey would do much of the political arm-twisting necessary to gain support in Congress. Johnson reached out to the Republican and Democratic leadership. He cautioned Republican leaders that if the Republicans fought this bill, they would be incurring the wrath of blacks and civil rights supporters for years to come. Johnson was utilizing all his political skills in his commitment to the civil rights package. There was no turning back.

The Civil Rights Act of 1964, if passed, would remake Southern society. Segregated hotels, restaurants, swimming pools, theaters, drinking fountains, and restrooms would eventually become a thing of the past as they would become outlawed by federal law. The bill would also provide federal protection against job and voting discrimination. Many Southern congressmen actively opposed the civil rights bill. Although President Johnson and Vice President Humphrey were able to guide the bill through the House of Representatives, the Senate posed a larger problem as the rules allowed its members to filibuster, a method of having Senate members speak continuously in order to prevent a vote. When a group of conservatives and segregationists did filibuster the bill, the coalition of Democrats and Republicans managed to break the delaying tactic and end the debate. The Civil Rights Act of 1964 was signed into law on July 2. Johnson had taken the gamble and won.

Based on my own beliefs and the encouragement of some very knowledgeable and enthusiastic teachers and parents, I decided to take a major risk on the grouping issue. I spoke to teacher groups and parent groups concerning this issue and the need for change. This change, since it involved policy, would have to be made by the school board. Still, I wanted the public to know that this was the direction that I was recommending to the school board because I believed, educationally, it was in the best interests of the children of Westborough. To me, this was one of the decisions where the superintendent could not be neutral. It went to the core of our belief as a school system as to the most appropriate way to deliver instruction. These types of decisions are why we are educational leaders.

At all meetings, I continually emphasized that this new grouping model did not lower standards for some students but rather raised standards for all. The question I would invariably get at each meeting was: How do you ensure in a class with mixed-ability students that the high-achieving students will not become bored while the students who already have academic difficulty will not become frustrated? I continually emphasized that even in a mixed-ability classroom, there had to be a recognition that students learned at different speeds, so we would encourage teachers, when appropriate, to depart from whole-group instruction to group the students within the classroom. This approach would allow for each group to be challenged. Unlike in the past, when grouping was rigid, the new grouping model would be flexible within the classroom so as to allow students to move freely between groups, depending on the skill being taught. With this approach, no longer would students be totally separated in different classes from other children based solely on ability or performance. To me, this system was fair for all children. Still, not everyone was convinced of the wisdom of this approach.

Although there was certainly no violence, some of the parents reacted with that same sense of disappointment that many Southerners felt with Johnson. The confrontation on this issue would be at the school board.

When the issue came up at school board, the meeting room was crowded, forcing some parents to stand. One parent had told me that for the sake of both groups, you had to separate students by ability. "You could not make chicken salads from chicken feathers," he said. I didn't know what that meant, but I did not like the sound of it. During the meeting, one parent asked how we could possibly think it was sound educationally to integrate the smart kids with the stupid kids. The chair of our committee, a strong supporter of heterogeneous grouping, tried to diffuse the volatility of this remark.

"Surely you don't mean to say some children are stupid."

"Yes I do," he remarked. "If we are to discuss this problem we must be realistic."

His comments set off an emotional debate. A mother jumped up and said, "My son has learning difficulties, but he is not stupid." Other parents challenged the statement until the issue died down. The school board agreed to a public meeting two weeks later.

The delay did not lessen the intensity of the debate. From the outset, I told people that I strongly opposed ability grouping because it locked students into certain sections based on achievement. At the public meeting, I spoke of the unfairness of ability grouping and the reasons for my beliefs. I emphasized how we value our students within the Westborough Public Schools and how we believe all children are capable of learning. I also stressed that any system we implemented would be designed to challenge all students and not to impede the progress of any.

That night in the auditorium was difficult as it was hard to persuade certain good, caring parents that their children would not be disadvantaged by mixed-ability grouping. We continued to assure pro-ability-grouping parents that we would encourage that ability grouping be used at times within the classroom at teacher discretion because we understood that there are learning differences among students. At the middle school, we also agreed that in grades seven and eight, ability grouping in math would be allowed. The alliance of the parents who favored mixed-ability grouping, certain concerned teachers, and me proved successful in making a convincing argument for the course we were to undertake. The school board formally adopted a policy of mixed-ability grouping in grades kindergarten through eight with exceptions in middle school math.

Even though the debate continued among the teachers, the overwhelming majority were willing to give the plan a chance. In meeting with the teachers, I promised to try to maintain reasonable class sizes and to immediately implement a staff-development program to address differentiated learning within the same classroom. Teachers would also be allowed to visit other school systems to observe strategies for working with mixed-ability classrooms. We would make it work.

Results

Lyndon Johnson took the risk, and both he and the country won a major victory. With the Civil Rights Act of 1964 and the strengthening of that bill one year later with the Voting Rights Act, America was moving forward to end segregation based on race. No longer would Southern segregation laws force blacks to be second-class citizens. Although prejudice and discrimination cannot simply be legislated away, at least blacks now had the legal foundation on which to build civil rights. The number of black voters and black officeholders would rapidly increase in the South. Lyndon Johnson, the former good-old-boy from Texas, had started a new era for the South.

There was certainly a down side for Johnson. As he had feared, civil rights would form a wedge in the Democratic Party. Many Southerners would soon desert the Democratic Party and move to the Republican Party. In fact, in Johnson's own presidential election in 1964, he lost the states of Arizona, Louisiana, Mississippi, Georgia, Alabama, and South Carolina. This was an omen of things to come as the Republican Party would eventually emerge as the dominant political force in the South.

How did Lyndon Johnson feel in retrospect about the risk? Johnson told historians that he was proud of what he had done. He said that he had completed what Lincoln had started. In 1973, when asked if he had any regrets, Johnson replied that he was ashamed that he had not done more.

The results in Westborough were also dramatic. In grades kindergarten through eight, we still have mixed-ability classes in the elementary and middle school where students are at times flexibly and temporarily grouped. It is difficult to assess the overall impact of this change. One thing does stand out. All of our students get the same high-quality instruction and have the same opportunities to be challenged. There is also no longer the stigma imposed on young children of being a permanent member of a segregated, low group. There is no doubt that if I had it to do over again, I would. I believe the best advice on risk was given by Mark Twain:

Twenty years from now you will be more disappointed by the things you didn't do than by the ones you did do. So throw off the bowlines. Sail away from the safe harbor. Catch the trade winds in your sails. Explore. Dream. Discover.

Reflection Points

- Risk taking is a key ingredient for effective leadership. By leaving the classroom to become an administrator, you have already begun to establish yourself as a risk taker. Continue to trust your own judgment.

- If failure is not a distinct possibility, there is no risk. The higher the probability of failure, the greater the risk you incur. Likewise, the greatest risks often yield the greatest gains for the students.
- You will fail in taking certain risks. This is part of the process of becoming an effective leader. Learn from your mistakes. No one expects you to bat a thousand.
- Before taking a risk, analyze the potential benefits as compared to the costs. Make sure to include personal costs in your equation. Sometimes saying no is the most appropriate course of action if the potential gain is not worth the gamble.
- Don't waffle. If you commit to a course of action, follow through unless there is compelling new evidence that convinces you of the need to withdraw.
- Sometimes the thought of embarrassment is a hindrance to willingness to take a chance. No one likes to see him- or herself ridiculed. However, do not allow fear to dictate your actions.
- Risks should align with your vision and personal philosophy. People will look for consistency in their leaders. Your actions should match your words.

CHAPTER FIVE

Negotiations

Does any superintendent of schools in the United States enjoy teacher negotiations? I don't. The situation is usually adversarial and unpleasant. Here I sit on the school board side of the bargaining table across from the teachers who look at me like I am a Benedict Arnold. For, on one hand, I ask teachers to continually sacrifice for the good of the children in the school system while, on the other hand, it appears to them that I am insensitive to their personal need for salary and benefit increases. As I sit at the table trying to look relaxed, I feel like explaining to the teachers, "You know, I really don't enjoy this at all."

Sometimes the school board and I are haggling with the teacher team over as little as a 0.25 percent increase in the contract base. For some teachers, that amounts to $100. I often feel very small during the proceedings, especially if I have negotiated a significant raise for myself. It's almost like I'm saying, "The school system can afford a sizable raise for me but not for you." However, pay raises for teachers are seldom a black-and-white issue. The school board faces a lot of pressure to bring in a contract that the taxpayers consider reasonable. An additional 1 percent salary increase for Westborough teachers translates into another $200,000 added to the budget, so even a fraction of that amount is a significant sum.

After one recent negotiations session, a veteran music teacher spoke to me in my office.

"Steve, you know the school board offer is not fair."

"Betty, these are tough times."

"Tough times, yes, but the school board offer is an insult to every teacher who works hard in this district. Anyhow, every time we come in to negotiate, the school board says it is a tough year. We just don't believe them anymore."

Betty had a valid point. Every bargaining year, we do use the same argument about affordability to the town. Even when the economy is prospering, every effort is made to limit salary raises as salaries make up almost 80 percent of the school budget.

"I agree that teachers are underpaid, but it is a national problem, not just a Westborough issue."

"Steve, if you know we are underpaid, why don't you switch to our side of the table and speak your true belief? That would be courage."

"No, Betty, that would not be helpful to anyone. Remember, I am still management, and I am a part of the school committee team."

That dialogue illustrates the plight of the superintendent. The teachers bristle at seeing us on the other side of the bargaining table. At the same time, the school board expects us to remain loyal during the process and to follow their direction for the negotiations. The fact that the school board is our employer certainly removes any doubt about our loyalty.

When I first became a superintendent, I would emphasize to the teacher bargaining team at the outset of negotiations that I was working in concert with the school board. This made for an immediately adversarial relationship with the teachers team. During tough bargaining, the teachers were usually standoffish toward me, although not outright hostile. I do make it a point to be visible in the schools during these times to demonstrate to the teachers that, in spite of an adversarial atmosphere, we all still have a job to do together. For the same reason during the negotiations process, I try to be very visible in the community.

Prior to serving as a superintendent of schools, I learned about community reaction to negotiations in rural New Hampshire. In 1976, as a young principal, I attended my first town meeting. One of the topics was funding of the recently resolved teacher contract. The chairman of the school board told the town meeting that the contract settlement was good for the town. This prompted Otis Johnson, an older farmer with deep roots in the community, to question the school board chair. "What are the salary terms of the contract?"

"The contract provides teacher raises of 10 percent over three years," the chairman answered calmly.

"You know, when I run the numbers with my calculator, I get 12 percent over three years."

"I hear what you are saying, Otis," the chair replied, "but we are really talking about only 10 percent over three years on the base. Additional monies for steps and lanes for teachers are included in every contract."

"So, the actual settlement is 12 percent," Mr. Johnson reiterated.

At this point, the union president rose to add to the discussion. "Maybe I can clarify the discrepancy. The raise is a 10 percent increase on the base. However, because teaching is a low-paying profession, teachers are rewarded each year for length of service to the district, which is called steps, and additional educational courses, which are called lanes."

"I understand," Otis Johnson persisted, "but you are still getting 12 percent over three years."

"Yes and no," the union president replied. "Remember, the steps and lanes are already built into the contract. We are only getting 10 percent on the base over three years."

The old farmer then cut to the chase. "Let's simplify this. How much more will you have in your pocket after three years then you have now?"

No one responded. He had made his point. Still, in spite of the protests of Mr. Johnson and several of his supporters, the budget, which included funding for the teacher raises, was approved by the town meeting. However, the perception of Mr. Johnson is common for certain people in all towns. There are usually questions about the teacher contract as school salaries are a large part of the town budget. People see the salary raises for teachers as related to their tax increases and perceive them as being taken directly from their pockets.

School boards nationwide confront public pressure to keep teacher salary raises as moderate as possible. In many towns, school board members are friendly with members of other town boards and the Republican and Democratic town committees. They want to demonstrate to these people that they are fiscally prudent and capable of holding the line on raises. This causes them to sometimes set unreasonable expectations and assume a tougher bargaining position than might be warranted.

Another problem with negotiations is when the school board does not take the advice of the superintendent. In Westborough, my school board members willingly accept and often defer to my expertise in the areas of curriculum and instruction. However, I can tell that they sometimes think I am soft when it comes to negotiations. Whenever I hear, "Steve, I'm going to show you how negotiations are done in the business world," I cringe. It often means hardball and a long, drawn-out bargaining process, producing no better results than if a more moderate position had been taken initially.

Of course, the teachers, like the school board, often prepare for bargaining with unreal expectations. The process with the teachers usually begins with some type of meeting between the teachers' negotiating team and the staff. At this meeting, the teachers establish high expectations and expect to make up for salary agreements from prior contracts, which they perceive as being too low. Many times, negotiating teams accept and present all teacher demands rather than saying no to any of their colleagues. The length and complexity of the initial teacher package can send the message that there is no real desire for a settlement to the school board. When this happens, you have two groups entering negotiations in an adversarial environment.

During the negotiations, the school board does have many resources on its side, such as the unlimited services of the superintendent and school attorney. Frequently, it is also supported by other town officials. The school board is the elected representative of the community and, as such, has the power to speak for the community. When it discusses the financial hardship of the town, it has credibility with the community as its members also pay the taxes needed to support town services. Many people who are concerned with rising taxes appreciate a strong stand by the school board to limit teacher salary increases. The school board also has the power to approve any raises, although the funding for the raises is contingent on town meeting approval.

The teachers also have advantages that pose a challenge to the school board. Parents often support the teachers. After all, these people serve their children, and they are often the subject of dinner conversation. How can you dislike the kindly first-grade teacher who teaches your child how to read? Many people believe teachers are underpaid, and there is an amount of sympathy that people have for teachers.

Teachers have strategies at their disposal that they can translate into leverage. They can make the negotiations highly visible and portray the superintendent and school board as unfair and unbending. No school board or superintendent enjoys being in the limelight and appearing heavy-handed with teachers. Teachers can also blame the superintendent if negotiations appear to break down. In several local districts during negotiations, the teachers voted no confidence in the superintendent. The public may understand that the superintendent can be a lightning rod for teacher dissatisfaction with the bargaining. However, votes of no confidence certainly are hurtful to superintendents as they increase the criticism from our detractors. Such a move personalizes the conflict and sets up the superintendent as the person responsible for the deadlock.

Teachers also have the weapon of job action. This can vary from working only to the letter of the contract to, in extreme cases, striking. As a young teacher, I was involved in a strike and can remember how divisive this was for the faculty. Ten years later, I remember returning to that town as high school principal and still hearing an argument between two teachers over their role in the strike twenty years before. In most states, teacher strikes are illegal. However, that does not mean they are impossible, and in Massachusetts during the last decade, there have been several teacher strikes, which make this threat a reality.

Entering into our recent negotiations, I wanted to build goodwill on both sides to have productive bargaining as Jimmy Carter did in the Israeli-Egyptian peace negotiations of 1978.

The Challenge

As a student of Middle Eastern history, President Jimmy Carter understood the complexity of negotiating a settlement for that region. The Middle East was one of the world's political hot spots, and the leaders of Israel and the Arab world would not even speak to each other. In particular, there had been animosity between the Jewish people and Egypt, which dated back to biblical times. The enmity between the sides was intense. There was an absence of trust on both sides.

The Arab states viewed the Israelis as colonialists who captured Arab territory, displaced their populations, occupied the land, and put up settlements to intensify their hold on their conquests. They believed that Israel kept the best land and water resources to construct Jewish settlements, while relegating many of the Arab residents to subsistence farming on inferior land. This caused further strain between Israel and its neighbors.

The Israeli perception was different. They viewed the Arabs as aggressors who had tried unsuccessfully to wipe out the Jewish state militarily four times. They witnessed the Arabs' continual refusal to recognize Israel's right to exist, and they heard the threats of the Arab world about destroying the state of Israel. The Israelis had to also face the issue of Arab terrorism, which posed a threat to the Israeli population. The animosity ran deep between the two groups.

President Carter was interested in facilitating the peace process through his direct involvement. However, Carter's advisors warned him about being personally engaged in the negotiations. This area of the world was highly volatile, and the possibility of an Egyptian-Israeli agreement was remote. Presidential advisors cautioned him that he did not need a foreign policy failure to mark his administration. In spite of the obvious difficulties, President Carter was intrigued by the possibility of brokering an agreement between the belligerents.

Preparing for the most recent Westborough teacher negotiations, as superintendent I wanted to create the trust that would make successful negotiations possible. This was not easy as our history in the system had been problematic. The prior negotiations had taken eighteen months to complete and were filled with acrimony and distrust. During the process, the teachers would march into their respective school buildings together to show solidarity with the teacher bargaining team. During one school board meeting, approximately two hundred teachers marched in to let the school board and the administration know of their unhappiness over the progress of the negotiations. On two occasions, when an agreement was forged between the school board and the bargaining team, the teachers voted down the proposed contract and eventually replaced their own bargaining team with a more militant group. When the teachers finally ratified a later proposal, the agreement passed by only one vote, 197–196.

I had suggested to the teachers prior to the current negotiations that we engage in interest-based bargaining, also called win-win bargaining. In this approach, both sides try to work together to discuss issues and develop possible solutions. Several negotiations before, we had tried this approach, and the contract was settled over a weekend. The reaction to my proposal for interest-based bargaining from the teachers was negative. They believed that the school board had intentionally dragged its feet during the last negotiations in an attempt to wear down the teachers through prolonged bargaining. If I was looking for their trust, the teachers were not interested.

The school board also was not willing to show the flexibility necessary for a quick settlement. At the request of the school board, I produced a list of recent settlements in the state. The school board felt all these settlements were excessive given the economic times. They believed that if we could show resolve in negotiations, we could do better. Economic conditions were difficult in Westborough, and the school board felt the teachers should be more understanding of the plight of the taxpayer.

The problems associated with all negotiations are quite similar. Each side feels that it is in the right and that the other side is being obstinate. Neither side usually listens well; nor does it set realistic expectations. What is particularly difficult about teacher negotiations is that schools are usually collegial systems, and the strife that sometimes accompanies negotiations becomes counterproductive to a good learning environment for students. Teacher morale often declines during difficult bargaining. They complain about being underappreciated, which only serves to worsen morale. Suddenly, negotiations, rather than students or instruction, become the topic of discussion among teachers.

How did Jimmy Carter develop a successful settlement, given the animosity between the two sides?

The Issues

Against the advice of his advisors, Carter committed himself personally to a leading role in facilitating Egyptian-Israeli peace negotiations. He arranged for President Anwar Sadat and Prime Minister Menachem Begin to meet with him at Camp David, the presidential compound in Maryland, to try to resolve the issues. Carter did not realize how complex these negotiations would be, and the meeting originally scheduled for three days extended to thirteen days.

President Carter tried to create the best possible conditions for success. There would be a press blackout so that the world would not know the status of negotiations. This would prevent grandstanding by representatives from both sides. It also prevented critics from sabotaging the discussions through negative reaction to the proposals. The negotiating teams were housed in cottages located close to each other, with golf carts, bicycles, and walking trails all available to facilitate contact between the two sides.

Even with these conditions, the atmosphere was tense. Begin and Sadat never developed a rapport, and they seldom spoke directly to each other. This animosity extended to their subordinates. Many of these men had fought against each other during the Arab-Israeli wars, and each blamed the other for the deaths of friends and relatives. This would be a difficult negotiation.

Both Sadat and Begin came to Camp David under enormous pressure not to make concessions. Sadat knew that all Arab leaders were watching him, and he realized that if he made concessions to Israel to secure a peace, these leaders would accuse him of selling out. He was respected by the Arab leaders as head of the strongest and most populous Arab country and as the man who had led his country into war with Israel in 1972. By attending this conference with Israeli leaders, he was now under intense criticism from the Arab world. Critics in Syria, Iraq, and Libya had even called for his assassination for participating in any talks with the Israelis. These threats were taken seriously as King Abdullah I of Jordan had been assassinated for talking about the possibility of peace with Israel over twenty-five years before.

Prime Minister Begin also had to confront the fears of the skeptics of the peace discussions. He was a hero in Israel for his role in the fight for independence. He had been a leader in the guerilla organization that had worked to drive the British from Palestine. After independence, Begin established a major political party, Likud, which took a very hard line against returning land to the Arabs. Many people in Israel expected him to hold strong on issues of security and not accede to Egyptian or even American demands. The issues themselves were difficult to grapple with. Sadat demanded that Israel agree to withdraw all military forces and civilian settlers from the Sinai Peninsula, which had been Egyptian territory before the wars. This demand was nonnegotiable. He also wanted autonomy for the Palestinian people in the West Bank and Gaza as these areas were then under military occupation by Israel.

Conversely, Begin believed that returning the Sinai to Egypt would be a huge mistake as Egypt could then amass armies on the Sinai Peninsula and eventually attack Israel again. In addition, Sinai was now part of Israel, and it contained strategic airfields and also provided oil for Israeli factories. Begin also saw Palestinian autonomy as a threat since the Palestinians could use their freedom to invite other Arab nations to attack Israel through their territory. Getting agreement on these emotional issues would be a true test of Carter's diplomatic skills.

What lessons could I learn from President Jimmy Carter to resolve my crisis in Westborough? His personal qualities of patience, courage, perseverance, and willingness to take risks could certainly serve as an inspiration. Like President Carter, I was engaged with two sides who felt strongly that their positions were justifiable. Although the major issues were not as volatile as those of Sinai and the Palestinians, they were still important to the participants. I sat through the school board deliberations, so I knew the key issues were salary and insurance. The town was having financial issues due to a downturn in the economy, and it would be difficult to justify raises to a town that was seeing large tax increases and experiencing increasing unemployment.

What complicated the negotiations issue even further was that the school board wanted to grant no raises in year one of a three-year pact, and it wanted a union give back on the issue of insurance. The town paid 90 percent of the annual insurance premium for one of our insurance providers, and the school board wanted to decrease that to 75 percent. The cost of health insurance was soaring, rising at rates of 20 percent per year for the last two years. The school board planned on asking the teachers to assume a portion of the increased cost.

All I could think was, Here we go again; another contentious negotiation was about to begin. Like President Carter, I initially faced a strong resistance to compromise. I told the school board that a proposal that called for no raise in year one and a reduction of benefits would be a difficult sell to the teachers. I urged the school board to have flexibility by developing backup plans for their bargaining team. In response, I received that "Steve, you are a bit too soft" look from some of the members as they ignored my advice. It was very easy for the school board to discuss needed union concessions before the actual bargaining had begun. The committee did not consider that the union was looking for this to be a good negotiations year for them and thus was not thinking of concessions that might have to be made on their part.

At the initial meeting, the union negotiating team presented its package to the school board team, which included two school board members, me, my two assistants, and the school attorney. First, the teachers talked about the fine job they had done with the children and our high test scores on standardized tests. They stressed that now was the time for the town to recognize their efforts through a significant salary increase. The bargaining team emphasized how, traditionally, teaching has been an underpaid profession, and it was time for the town to address the issue.

The teacher team also presented thirty-five different proposals, ranging from financial items, such as higher stipends for activities and a new salary schedule for nurses, to contractual language changes, such as the time that teachers could leave school at the end of the day. Our current contract required teachers to remain for an additional forty-five minute period following the student dismissal bell. This forty-five minute provision in the contract was irritating to the teachers. They emphasized that it was both unprofessional and unnecessary since, they maintained, they would stay after school to help children even if there were no contractual obligation.

The teacher proposal met with an initial silence from the school board, then a series of questions seeking clarification. Their proposal was more aggressive and unrealistic than the school board representatives or I had envisioned. Luckily, no one on either team used any language that could be considered inflammatory by the other side, so at least both sides were still talking to each other. How could I as superintendent bridge the gap?

Strategy, Solution, and Compromise

President Carter lobbied both sides hard. He met with Begin and Sadat separately as he felt both trusted him but did not trust each other. He leveraged both by saying the world would blame the side who would not be flexible enough to work toward peace. He threatened both sides with loss of American support. Jimmy Carter proved a good listener and tried to address the concerns of both sides. Of course, where there is no trust, it is difficult to negotiate. However, he altered his strategy in his approach to each side.

With the Egyptians, his strategy was to meet privately with Anwar Sadat to advocate flexibility, and he had less contact with his advisors. Most of the Egyptian advisors were more rigid and felt Sadat was extending himself too much. To Sadat, he spoke of a historic opportunity missed if the Egyptian president had taken the bold step of coming to Camp David but was unwilling to reach a compromise. He continually emphasized to Sadat that, without peace, the Middle Eastern struggle would continue indefinitely, with each side experiencing loss of life.

However, when urging compromise to the Israelis, President Carter would use a different strategy. As Prime Minister Begin relied on the counsel of his advisors, President Carter would use them as intermediaries with the Israeli prime minister. He or his advisors would often visit with Ezer Weitzman, the Israeli defense minister, and Ahoud Barak, the Israeli attorney general, as both of these men were trusted by Begin and tended to take a more flexible position. They would then explore alternatives with Begin.

Finally, after thirteen days of meetings, both sides agreed to compromise, and an agreement was finally forged. Israel agreed to return Sinai to the Egyptians and to dismantle all Israeli settlements in the area. A plan was also developed for Palestinian autonomy at a future time. Egypt agreed to recognize Israel, to exchange ambassadors, and to drop all trade restrictions. At Camp David, both Begin and Sadat signed the two historic documents, a Framework for Peace in the Middle East and a Framework for the Conclusion of a Peace Treaty between Egypt and Israel.

In Westborough, following the first session of negotiations at which no progress was made, I met privately with our local union president to see where we were going and where there was room for compromise. As Jimmy Carter had demonstrated, bargaining discussions are best done away from the table, where the atmosphere is much more relaxed.

I asked her, "OK, what will it take to settle the contract?"

"Steve for a settlement, which is sellable to our membership, we need 9 percent over three years, no change in insurance, and the dropping of the forty-five minute requirement for teachers to remain after the student dismissal bell."

"Sorry, I can't deliver that," I responded. "Nine is far too high and the forty-five minutes is really nonnegotiable from both the school board's point of view and mine. That forty-five-minute provision guarantees extra help for students after school, and we are not about to trade it away." I felt about compromising on the forty-five minutes the same way that President Sadat felt about relinquishing control of Egyptian land to the Israelis.

"Steve, all right, 9 percent may not be realistic, but the school board's offer of 5 percent over three years is far too low. We would be responsive to a more realistic pay increase proposal, even if it was not at the 9 percent level. We can also drop the demand on the forty-five minutes. However, we will not compromise on the issue of teachers' paying higher insurance premiums."

I believed her position was quite reasonable. However, this did not surprise me as she was usually a realistic person who looked for solutions rather than problems. Some of the members of her bargaining team were more unrealistic. From our conversation, it was clear to me that attempting to negotiate teacher concessions on insurance would be problematic. The area of teacher flexibility would only be on salary demands. However, how was I going to sell it to the school board? One of the two people on the school board negotiating team was an insurance salesman who correctly believed that increased health insurance costs were among the biggest reasons the town budget was increasing at such a rapid rate. The school board also knew the selectmen would probably ask police, fire, and public works to pay an increased share of insurance premiums to help the town financially. If the school board could gain concessions in this area, they would be setting the direction for negotiations for the rest of the town departments.

I told the union president, "Your demands are not unreasonable. Give me some time." At the school board strategy session the next week, the committee was fired up. One member stated well the viewpoint of the entire school board. "Taxes are skyrocketing in this town. We have to draw the line in the sand. This insurance concession is a must for a settlement." I agreed that insurance concessions would be important to relieve the pressure on town finances, but with the possibility of no raise for next year, this demand would make an agreement almost impossible.

As the tone of the meeting began to take on a fervid, uncompromising tone, I realized that my urging for compromise had had little immediate impact on their thinking. The school board was developing unrealistic proposals. Still, in spite of frustration, it is important that the superintendent provide an opinion on the fairness of school board and teacher proposals. The superintendent has to be the catalyst to move along the process. He or she has to evaluate the proposals from the teachers and make recommendations to the school board. The school board on its own has a difficult time agreeing to proposals from the union as it often sees the union as merely self-serving. What the school board had to understand is that unions are self-serving, or they would not be reflecting the interest of the teachers who support the union through annual dues.

When the two bargaining teams met again, the session was unproductive as neither side would move during what both parties perceived to be an absence of both good faith and flexibility by the other side. Finally, an impasse was declared, and a mediator was brought in.

I like to have a mediator involved when one or both sides continues to posture instead of moving toward an agreement. President Carter used Ezer Weitzman, the Israeli defense minister, and Ahoud Barak, the attorney general, to effectively mediate issues with the Israeli prime minister Menachem Begin and bring forth a softening of the Israeli position.

Appointment of a mediator can be a positive communications vehicle. The school board is able to hear a realistic appraisal of its position from a neutral party who has experience working with school boards in other towns. This gives committee members a better perspective on what is fair. The teachers' association team gets the benefit of hearing about the settlements in other towns and receiving feedback from a neutral party, which makes the team more realistic in its demands. The teacher bargaining team can also later explain to its membership that the mediator worked with both sides to create the conditions for a fair settlement. As I had worked with this mediator before, I was confident that we could finally drop the pretenses and move forward.

The first mediation session went fairly well as both sides appeared to like the mediator. There seemed to be hope. However, neither side made any meaningful concessions. Still, there was agreement to meet again as both parties felt a new optimism.

During the second mediation session, one of the two school board members of the negotiating team was unable to attend, and I knew that this presented an opportunity to move. After spending the first hour with the teacher team, the mediator felt that a money settlement could be worked out to the school board's satisfaction with close to a zero salary increase in year one, but to get a settlement, the school board would have to drop its demand for higher insurance premiums for teachers.

The one remaining school board member in attendance, Jack Wilson, sold insurance for a living, so to get him to move off this demand would be difficult. However, he was a very reasonable person who was a former teacher himself, and he was sympathetic to teacher issues. I pushed him hard for resolution, maybe too hard, but not nearly as hard as Carter had pushed Begin and Sadat. He appeared a bit agitated by the pressure that I was exerting, so I backed off a bit to let him think the issue through. However, with the mediator and school lawyer on one side of him and me and my two assistants on the other side all urging compromise, after an hour and a half of discussion, I could hear his position shifting.

Finally, I said to him, "Jack, let's drop the insurance demand and call it a day." At this point, I believed the offer on the table was fair to both sides.

He responded with a bit of irritation in his voice. "Steve, you are the best negotiator the teachers have."

The mediator quickly followed my lead. "Jack, this is a fair deal, and it is at the raise you have already agreed to."

I kept the pressure on. "Jack, if we say no, all it will do is prolong negotiations. This is a reasonable compromise. Negotiations for another six months won't solve anything, and it will put the district into turmoil."

I could see by his face and body language that he, too, was now seeing this as a fair resolution.

"I'm still not happy, but I'll agree to keep the process moving. Still, it must go back to the entire school board for approval."

With the agreement having the tentative approval of both bargaining teams, settlement became a possibility.

Results

Although there was strong resistance to the negotiated frameworks in Israel and throughout the Arab world, a treaty was signed in Washington by Prime Minister Begin and President Sadat in 1979. The result of the Camp David negotiations was an end to the open hostility between Egypt and Israel. Israel received the diplomatic recognition and end to the economic boycott that it so badly wanted. Egypt recovered all the land lost in the Sinai, and it secured a framework for Palestinian autonomy in the West Bank. With Egypt no longer a belligerent against Israel, there would be a greater possibility for peace in the Middle East. That peace between Egypt and Israel still exists, but the relations are cold. The issue of the Palestinians' autonomy has still not been resolved.

In Westborough, the reaction of both sides was similar to the reaction of the Arabs and Israelis to Camp David. Some people on both sides criticized the compromise, although each side ratified the contract. Compromises are often perceived as unsatisfactory as they do not meet the expectations of victory that each side had hoped for. Certain community members criticized the school board for not extracting concessions on insurance before settling the contract. This became a greater issue when the police, fire, and public works departments' unions all agreed to increase their own insurance contributions.

Several teachers criticized the negotiating team for bringing back an unsatisfactory money settlement. Still, both the teachers and the school board did ratify the contract. One week after the negotiations concluded, a group met in the middle school to begin the plans for the next negotiations. These teachers felt that they had not received a fair contract, and they wanted to prepare for the next round of negotiations, which was almost three years away.

I was just happy that the process yielded a fair agreement so that the Westborough Public Schools could again focus on its primary role, the education of children.

Reflection Points

- Productive conversations are often best held privately with the union leadership to gain an understanding of teacher priorities before negotiations begin and throughout the process.
- When setting ground rules for bargaining with the union bargaining team, include a provision limiting statements to the press. Negotiating is an emotional process, and inflammatory remarks to the press may fire up the community and teachers and make resolution more difficult.
- Successful negotiation is based on flexibility and compromise. Still, negotiations should not mean surrender. Develop carefully with the school board your proposals before you begin negotiating.
- In the event of job action by the teachers, such as work-to-rule, exercise patience and restraint in your public comments. Do not allow yourself or the members of the school board to be provoked. Caution the school board not to unnecessarily exacerbate ill feeling by using offensive remarks, such as that teaching is only a part-time job. Attacking the teaching profession is an unproductive strategy as it will only make settlement more difficult.
- Remember, after negotiations, you will have to work with the teachers. Civility and respect are key components of any negotiations.
- A mediator can be helpful when bargaining is not progressing, and negotiations move toward an impasse. A mediator may offer a valuable third-party perspective and may also serve to diffuse pent up emotion.

- During bargaining do not take anything personally. Negotiations are usually about money and contract language and not about you. Yes, it stings if your leadership style is criticized and linked to low morale in the school system. Still, airing problems with the superintendent is not an unusual union strategy to try to draw sympathy from the school board.
- Stay visible in the schools during the process. In spite of the contentiousness of collective bargaining, it's important for the superintendent to continue to provide visible leadership to the school system.
- Successful strategies in teacher negotiations can be applied to grievance resolutions or any type of dispute needing compromise.
- Remember the words of John Fitzgerald Kennedy: "We cannot negotiate with those who say, what's mine is mine and what is yours is negotiable."

CHAPTER SIX

Communication

"And what is the recommendation of our superintendent?" the school board chair asks in a solemn voice. The room becomes quiet. All eyes turn to you to espouse the wisdom needed to clarify the issue. Even though you might not have expected this particular topic to arise, as superintendent, you must always be ready to provide information on educational issues. Is this fair? Even quiz show hosts give contestants a few seconds to collect their thoughts before they answer, and they usually have the opportunity to ask the host to repeat the question. The superintendent gets no such luxury. The public expects you to be aware of everything in the district from the changes in the Advanced Placement physics curriculum to why some immature senior was snapping wet towels at the freshmen in the boys' locker room. At the school board meeting or at any public meeting, no matter how complex the question, there is an expectation that you will have a timely, well-thought-out, comprehensive answer. Sometimes an acceptable response is, "I'd be happy to study the situation and come back to the school board at the next meeting with a full report and recommendation." That type of answer does allow you some time to collect your thoughts. However, more often than not, the school board wants to know your opinion immediately. As superintendent, you speak for the school system, and people in the district do want to know your opinion on crucial issues. Communication skills are a necessity for an effective superintendent.

Communication has two vital components. The first is connectivity, the ability to connect with the public, and the second is substance, the ability to convey a worthwhile message. If a superintendent only has the quality of connectivity, people will eventually look at him as being shallow and irrelevant. If a superintendent lacks connectivity but has an important message, the message may be lost on his audience, who may come to view him as aloof and ineffective.

The ancient Greeks well knew the importance of connectivity as related in the story of Cassandra. Cassandra, according to Greek mythology, was given the gift of prophecy by the sun god, Apollo. However, because she did not respond to his overtures of affection, Apollo put a curse on her that made people disbelieve anything she said. Cassandra warned the Trojans that it was a poor idea to bring the wooden horse into the walls of Troy as it housed Athenian soldiers who would destroy the city. People did not listen to her warning, and Troy fell when the Greek soldiers hidden within the horse opened the door of the city to the waiting Greek Army. What superintendent has not felt like Cassandra? We don't have the gift of prophecy, but we do sometimes bear the curse of disbelief, especially when we advocate for unpopular issues, such as the need for increased funding for schools through higher taxes. The question is how we connect effectively to win the trust of the community and staff.

President John F. Kennedy learned the importance of connectivity during the time of the Bay of Pigs invasion of Cuba in 1961. President Kennedy had given the false hope of significant American support to a group of armed Cuban exiles who attempted to overthrow Cuban leader Fidel Castro. This resulted in failure and the total defeat of the exile army.

Kennedy freely admitted that he had misjudged the Cuban situation, and he took full responsibility for the failed mission. Although the incident was an international embarrassment for the United States, the American public respected President Kennedy for being forthright and truthful in his explanation to them. Americans connected with a president who demonstrated that he was human and capable of making errors.

Poll numbers showed widespread support for the president. People began to trust John Kennedy as someone who could be honest with the public. When he learned of the positive public reaction to his admission, a shocked Kennedy commented, "The worse I do, the more popular I get." This connectivity is crucial to the credibility of a leader. People judge a school administrator on factors such as approachability, honesty, and commitment to children. We all tend to view ourselves as having these necessary qualities, but it is important that the public perceive us in this same way. As I have always considered myself a good communicator, I was surprised when I erred in not connecting with Westborough parents on an important topic. The case involved a bomb scare at the middle school. In a time of violence in our nation's schools, I should have handled the situation in a more effective manner.

On a mild spring day, the principal of the Westborough Middle School telephoned to tell me that a child had scratched the words "A bomb will go off tomorrow" onto a gym locker. I immediately stopped what I was doing and drove to the middle school. The principal and I both examined the locker and noticed that the scratches were barely legible. It must have been done in a hurry to avoid detection. We both believed the seventh grader who reported it was probably the perpetrator. Who else could have even read this scrawling on the locker?

I advised the principal to call the police and have an officer there in the morning when the buses arrived. I felt that the threat was minimal, but I would still take precautions.

The next day, I received a flood of angry parental calls as many students had related the incident to their parents. Parents were outraged that with the school violence sweeping the country, the administration had neglected to tell them about the threat, and they viewed this as negligence. Many parents had chosen not to send their children to school that day because of the threat. As the phone calls continued, I decided to send a letter to all middle school parents in which I explained my actions and that of the middle school principal. I also invited parents to meet with me in the school auditorium to discuss this issue. To ensure that all went well, I invited the police chief, the fire chief, and the middle school principal to serve on a panel with me to talk about how the incident was handled and how all precautions were taken to ensure student safety.

The evening proved to be a disaster with parent after parent expressing anger and frustration that they were not alerted to the threat. It was one of those meetings where I continually looked at the clock, hoping the evening would end before the crowd became more hostile. On reflection, I now realize that the lack of notification was not the real problem. The issue was that I had failed to see parents as partners. I treated the problem as routine, while the parents would later see it as serious. Because of this difference, I could not connect with the parents who saw me that night as callous, insensitive, and unconcerned about the safety of children. Still, that evening meeting was valuable as it demonstrated to me that parents wanted more than a capable administrator. They wanted an empathetic leader who understood their fears and responded to them in a way they considered appropriate.

The second component in communication is the message. What do you stand for as superintendent? People expect that you will advocate for children, foster a safe, nurturing environment, and provide quality education. A leader must stand for something, and your messages communicate to the public what that is.

One of the reasons Franklin Delano Roosevelt was successful as president was that he could convey powerful messages, and he had concrete plans to translate those messages into action. People do not want to hear only what the problem is. Often they already know what the problem is, as they are sometimes disheartened and frustrated during crises. They look for their leaders to provide affirmation of their feelings and solutions to the problems.

When Franklin Roosevelt was inaugurated in 1933, America was in the midst of the Great Depression. There was a sharp decline in business and agriculture and widespread unemployment. Roosevelt, in his inaugural speech, delivered to all Americans a powerful message of hope.

First of all, let me assert my firm belief . . . that the only thing we have to fear is fear itself—nameless, unreasoning, unjustified terror which paralyzes needed efforts to convert retreat into advance.

Roosevelt told Americans that he would begin a massive government employment program that would provide them with jobs and build up

America's resources. This is what the public wanted to hear from their president. They already knew how bad conditions were. They wanted to know what he would do to make things better. On a smaller scale, the public wants to know what we as superintendents stand for and what our plan is. Day-to-day administration will not inspire the public and gain us the support we need. I know my confidence swells when I deliver a strong, consistent message. I feel the message reflects who I am as superintendent, and it demonstrates my belief system. This gives me the confidence to face the public and my own staff. When politics intervene, the message can become weakened or garbled, because without my own personal commitment, I cannot expect others to follow my leadership. Ronald Reagan is an outstanding example of a president who had the ability to connect with the public and to deliver powerful messages.

Connecting

How many superintendents have the communications background of a Ronald Reagan? Most of us have spent our whole career in classrooms or school offices with only occasional contact with the public. Reagan had the unique opportunity to hone his communication skills as a movie actor and as a television personality. Ronald Reagan had also toured the country as a spokesman for General Electric (GE), and he visited GE plants across the country talking about the greatness of America. Reagan became very relaxed when speaking to people and came across as very genuine and compassionate. Later, as a politician, he connected quite easily with people as he had years of experience addressing audiences.

President Reagan connected with Americans through his aura of confidence, humility, humor, and optimism. Economic times were tough when Reagan first entered office, with high inflation and widespread unemployment. In his first inaugural address, he said that he would work to limit the role of government because his faith was in the American people to solve the economic issues confronting America. President Reagan projected a can-do attitude and a deep belief in America. Ronald Reagan connected to people because they viewed him as a strong leader who could restore America's confidence. To many Americans, President Ronald Reagan stood as a father figure who extolled God, country, and family.

Even adversity could not shake Reagan's resolve as he demonstrated courage and composure when John Hinckley Jr. attempted to assassinate him during his first year as president. News reports described to the public how the wounded president, with a bullet only an inch from his heart, walked from the presidential limousine into the hospital without any assistance. Stories circulated about how Reagan greeted the surgical team brought in to treat his wounds with the comment, "Please tell me you're Republicans." Likewise, people laughed at Reagan's response to his wife, Nancy, after surgery: "Honey, I forgot to duck." The public viewed Reagan as a courageous person without any pretension. His quick wit and humor showed him to be a man of the people. People look to their leaders to be unpretentious and able to relate to them. In essence, they want their leaders to project human qualities.

Humor often played an important role in Reagan's ability to connect with the public. During the election of 1984, President Reagan demonstrated the quick wit and self-deprecation that endeared him to the American public. During the first debate, Reagan appeared to stumble while his opponent Senator Walter Mondale of Minnesota looked sharp. In the press, there were many articles about Reagan's being too old to serve another term. Ronald Reagan's shining moment came in the second debate following a comment concerning his age. President Reagan replied, "I will not make age an issue of this campaign. I am not going to exploit for political purposes my opponent's youth and inexperience."

Even Mondale laughed at this response. Americans identified with the president's self-deprecating humor. Ronald Reagan's performance in the debate helped propel him to one of the largest presidential landslides in American history as he carried forty-nine states, while Mondale only carried his home state of Minnesota and the District of Columbia. People like their leaders to be able to smile, to laugh, and to show their human side. Reagan was one of the best at that.

As superintendent, I did not survive an attempted assassination or score points in a national debate. Nor had I been a famous actor. Still, there are things that can make a superintendent connect with the public and the teachers.

Visibility is very important to connecting with community members as people feel a sense of comfort and security in seeing their leader. Of course, the best method of connecting to the community is to move into the town. This will demonstrate to the public that you are a regular person who pays his taxes and contributes to the welfare of the town on a personal as well as a professional level. Although the strategy of establishing community residency can be helpful to the credibility of the superintendent, I personally rejected this strategy for two reasons. First, I do like my privacy, and I did not want to subject myself, my wife, and my children to the scrutiny that accompanies being a public official who lives in town.

The second reason I did not wish to live in town stemmed from my days as a New Hampshire principal. When I was hired as the high school principal in Lincoln, New Hampshire, I received an orientation from the chair of the school board. He informed me that if I moved into town, the expectation was that I would agree to have the school's boiler alarm installed in my house. It was explained to me that, in the event that the boiler shut down in the middle of the night, I would hear the alarm ringing, which was my signal to go to school to restart the boiler so that the building would have the necessary heat to conduct school in the morning. The chair felt that this was a very reasonable responsibility for a dedicated school administrator to execute given his concern for the safety and comfort of the children. I too felt it was a reasonable plan if someone other than I was responsible for waking up in the middle of the night to make sure the boiler was running. Right then and there, I decided that living in a neighboring district would be in the best interest of myself and my family, and as an administrator, I have never lived in the district in which I was employed.

As superintendent, although I chose not to live in Westborough, I did everything I could to connect with people by being very visible in the community. On a personal level, I worshiped in Westborough, joined a civic organization, and even shopped in town. I wanted the public to see me and relate to me as a person. I visited the schools daily, and parents and teachers could see that I was accessible, interested, and available. People like to see that the superintendent is on top of things and knows what is happening in the schools. I also went to sporting event and banquets. Any time the public was in the schools for an event, I tried to be there. The public wants the superintendent to show commitment by being visible and involved.

Early on, I tried to connect with the public during my first large athletic banquet. I knew this was an opportunity to show, like Reagan, that I could be a regular guy. Knowing that most people in high school were not super athletes, I saw this as a connection and told this story:

> Sometimes on snowy days, I go downstairs to my basement and look at the old high school trophies which have become tarnished with age. One shows a goalie with the letters "MVP" on the base. Another shows a basketball player with the word "Captain" inscribed on the statue, while a third shows a batter with the words "League All-Star" on the base.

I could see the crowd becoming agitated and thinking, boy this guy is into himself. Then I pulled a Reagan-type maneuver by saying,

> I'm proud of all those trophies. Unfortunately, they all belong to my wife, who is the athlete in our family. My only trophy is my perfect attendance pin for thirteen years in the Randolph Public Schools without an absence. Yes, I dressed for over two thousand consecutive homerooms. I was the Cal Ripken of the Randolph Public Schools.

Suddenly I could see the crowd loosen up and laugh. I knew I had connected well. Even Ronald Reagan, "The Great Communicator" himself, would have applauded that effort. A great danger to the superintendent is appearing to be arrogant. That story made me come across as being a leader who could poke fun at himself.

Like Reagan, I cultivated the regular-guy image while always taking care to maintain my personal dignity. I still cannot understand why the public enjoys seeing their school administrators engaging in activities with the students like donkey basketball games. I personally never enjoyed participating in this particular event where I would ride a donkey, as the donkey's spine is very hard and uncomfortable, and at times the donkey would not move at all, no matter what the prodding. Still, saying yes sends a positive "good sport" message to the community.

When the Harlem Rockets came to Westborough as a parent-teacher association fundraiser to play basketball against the faculty, the parents asked me to participate. I played and even jumped center against a seven footer. I gave it all my five-foot, seven-inch frame could deliver, but my performance was at best mediocre. Still, the parents loved it and cheered me on. At halftime, the daughter of the chair of the school asked for my autograph. In fact, I received more praise for playing in that game than for many of my educational initiatives. People want to see their superintendent as human, and like Reagan, I did whatever I could to keep connected.

Of course, connecting and giving meaningful messages can be two different things. Reagan was not considered "The Great Communicator" merely because he came across as likeable and strong to the public. Ronald Reagan was also admired because he stated very powerful messages that resonated with America, and he articulated plans for strong action.

Messages

Ronald Reagan made his messages simple and understandable. In foreign policy, the message was, the United States is a noble nation that stands up for democracy. You should be proud to be an American. We are the country that loves freedom and will protect it at any cost. The United States should not apologize for Vietnam or any attempts to fight communism anywhere in the world. President Reagan's message tapped into the patriotism and optimism of the United States. Reagan defined what America stood for, and people responded enthusiastically to his message.

To President Reagan, there was no compromise with the Soviets. Their system was bad and had to be changed. When Reagan called the Soviets "an evil empire," he believed it and conveyed that message to the American public. He told America that the Soviet leaders were liars and cheaters who had broken the treaties that they had signed with America. To Reagan, any treaty with the Soviets would require continual monitoring procedures to make sure the Soviets did not cheat again. Ronald Reagan stressed to the American public that the Soviets were heavily armed, and our best course of action was to meet their military challenge head on by building up our weapons systems.

President Reagan emphasized that he wanted peace and disarmament, but he would achieve it on our terms from a position of strength rather than through the failed policy of trusting the Soviets. Reagan made his position clear to the American public; the Soviets wanted world domination. His highest foreign policy priority would be to defeat communism. Reagan captured America's attention, but the question would be how he could turn rhetoric into action. The Soviet Union was a strong military power that was fomenting revolutions worldwide.

As President Reagan did, I tried to tap into this spirit of optimism to garner support for the school system. People want to believe in their schools and their children's teachers. Among my strong educational messages was the importance of modernizing our facilities. I stressed that Westborough was one of the best school systems in Massachusetts, but the school system needed improved facilities to maintain this level of educational excellence. Although the voters had already defeated a funding proposal for new schools, I remained optimistic. I continually sent the message that I understood new schools would be a large financial sacrifice for the townspeople, but the school system had always spent the money wisely, and new schools would be a sound investment for the town.

There were people who did not want to hear this message. New schools would mean a large increase in taxes. Critics pointed out that large school projects not only mean capital outlay for buildings but also additional funds for more staffing with more teachers, nurses, custodians, administrators, and other support staff. My message had to convey to the public that this type of expenditure was appropriate for the community and would pay dividends.

We were easily able to explain that as enrollment grew, class sizes would swell. However, there were people who were not convinced that class size alone would make a significant educational impact for the money spent. I continually heard the argument, Well, in my day, we had forty students in a class. I could relate to that as when I attended school in the 1950s and 1960s, we had large classes. Still, we continued to point out to the Westborough community that with technology and the hands-on methodologies, smaller classes were needed to make the system work most effectively. Another argument from the critics was that it is the teaching rather than the facility that makes the difference in the education of children. I always agreed that teachers make the difference. However new facilities would make our teaching staff even more effective as they would have the space and equipment they needed. Like Reagan, I tried to always remain courteous and respectful to the critics and not to personalize their opposition. My job was to explain to the public that we were currently hampered in our job by inadequate space. Lack of space meant more than just another child or two in a class. It was that our infrastructure was not adequate to meet the educational demands of the children of Westborough. Like Reagan, I tried to set a tone of optimism and explained what new facilities could offer. I described to parents how, in the elementary schools, our special education students and English-language learners, who were most easily distracted, were sometimes housed in the library behind partitions, in offices, or in storage closets. The string orchestra was practicing in the halls, while the art teacher was using a traveling cart that she wheeled from room to room. It wasn't just that the classes were larger, it was that there was not enough classroom space to provide for our programs. I explained at length how new facilities would solve these problems by creating the needed space.

The high school was a source of pride to the community. Built in 1968, the facility was state of the art for its time. However, many of the facilities, such as the library, auditorium, cafeteria, and laboratories, were now outdated. Like Reagan, I continually displayed optimism over what could be done in the future. Construction of new facilities for the high school would provide the space to allow us to expand programs to remain among the state leaders. Our award-winning music program would finally have adequate band, chorus, and orchestra rooms, while the drama program would have a modern auditorium in which to perform. Our science classes would have up-to-date labs. Our athletic and arts programs would have modern facilities, and the students would have a state-of-the-art library in which to do research.

I kept reiterating that a new high school would provide the technology that was so badly needed if we were looking to the future rather than just replicating the past. I used the example of how we had recently joined forty other schools worldwide in the virtual high school. Through the virtual high school, students were enrolling in courses ranging from a comparison of Eastern and Western philosophy to Advanced Placement statistics. Technology would yield new ways to learn, and Westborough must come on board or be left behind. The message of the need for improved facilities was easy to convey as most people did agree. The question became affordability.

Action Plan

President Reagan had a plan to implement his message. America would no longer coddle the Communists. Instead, the United States would strive to make them change the way that they did business. Reagan communicated to the American people that confronting the Soviet leadership would be his top foreign policy priority. Many Americans applauded Reagan's get-tough policy as finally someone was standing up to the Communists; others viewed him as a dangerous extremist. Ronald Reagan had campaigned for cutting taxes and cutting government spending. However, one area of spending that he increased dramatically was defense, where he instituted a set of proposals for new weapons systems.

Critics chastised the president for his priorities, and some referred to him as a warmonger. However Ronald Reagan did not personalize these attacks. Instead, he remained calm and continued to communicate with the American people concerning the needs for strong defense. Reagan would remind Americans that the Soviets did not honor treaties, so the United States should be ready to defend itself. Reagan even utilized humor to disarm his critics. When he was challenged about spending extravagantly on the B-1 bomber, Reagan replied, "How did I know it was an airplane? I thought it was vitamins for the troops."

President Reagan also emphasized to Americans that he did not agree with a live-and-let-live philosophy with the Russians. He advocated tough, straightforward talk to the Soviets, and Americans responded to this approach. Soviet premier Leonid Brezhnev had previously expounded the Brezhnev Doctrine, which implied that the Soviet military forces would be used to combat both internal and external efforts to convert a communist nation to capitalism. Reagan countered with his own position, which became known as the Reagan Doctrine: the United States would help insurgents in any country who sought to overthrow Communist rule. American military aid flowed into Afghanistan, Nicaragua, and Angola to finance anti-Communist movements. The Soviets now found themselves in a defensive position, trying to put down these worldwide insurgencies.

President Reagan could afford to talk tough as he knew from his advisors that, economically, the Soviet Union was crumbling, with its economy not growing. Reagan kept up the pressure, adding new advanced weapon systems and putting nuclear weapons into Europe. The Soviets were very concerned about Reagan's tough talk. Although many Americans liked their president's standing up to the Soviets, the Soviet leadership viewed Reagan as a dangerous person capable of bringing about war.

The central part of Reagan's defense plan was the Strategic Defense Initiative (SDI), or, as it was called by his critics, "Star Wars." This was a space-based missile defense system that would theoretically allow America to intercept Soviet rockets in space before they reached the United States. The Soviets feared this new system would allow America to be much more aggressive in its foreign policy since it could protect itself against Soviet reprisals.

President Reagan always communicated that he sought peace and not war. He did not want to bomb the Soviets; rather, he wanted them to change. When Mikhail Gorbachev came to power in the Soviet Union, Reagan believed this was a new type of Soviet leader whom he could work with. Still, in a series of meetings, Reagan talked of peace but still showed the same toughness as ever. He constantly told Gorbachev that Americans felt that Russia could not be trusted and that monitoring was the key to any agreement. Reagan talked publicly of eliminating all nuclear arms, but the bottom line was that America was continuing to build up weaponry, and Gorbachev knew the Russians could not compete. Although Reagan was willing to discuss eliminating certain types of nuclear weapons, the Star Wars program was not negotiable. Reagan was in a position of strength, which was widely applauded in the country.

The most direct challenge to Gorbachev happened on June 12, 1987, at the Berlin Wall. Here, Reagan communicated to the entire world where he stood: "Mr. Gorbachev, tear down this wall." As economic conditions worsened, the Soviets were in no position to continue the arms race. No other American president has stated his position on communism more forcefully. President Reagan knew the end of communism was near.

As superintendent, my plan was to build walls, not tear them down. Westborough needed new schools as there was no way we could maintain the same type of school system with such severe overcrowding. I unveiled a plan for $70 million for an addition/renovation to the high school and the construction of a large new elementary school.

There were critics who said that this type of expenditure was unacceptable, and we did not need to build a Mercedes where a Ford could do the job. Once before, the administration had brought forward a funding proposal for an expanded high school and a new elementary school to town meeting only to have the proposal resoundingly defeated. Like Reagan, I had to win support to make the plan successful.

To win approval, the administration would have to confront the four major issues that doomed the prior proposal:

1. Does enrollment justify new schools?
2. Are there other acceptable alternatives?
3. Can we afford the schools?
4. Would increased taxes drive out our senior citizens?

Critics constantly pointed out their belief that the overcrowding of the Westborough Public Schools was merely a temporary situation that would soon pass. They feared that if Westborough constructed new schools, the schools would later become depopulated, and the town would have made this large-scale investment for only a short-term solution. There was some logic to this argument as it is always possible that enrollment projections can be inflated. Even projecting enrollment figures more than five years out can be problematic as demographic conditions can change under conditions such as a downturn in the economy, which makes houses less affordable for families. Working with the town's building committee, we analyzed Westborough's demographic data from three different independent sources. The analysis revealed that even if Westborough's enrollment did not grow, and we merely maintained the number of students we had, our schools would remain overcrowded for at least ten years.

We also reviewed every reasonable solution to the overcrowding problem that was brought to us by the public. The most common and simplistic solution was installing portable classrooms adjacent to existing buildings. We did a complete analysis to show that not only would portables not solve the problems, but we had no place to adequately site the portables as our school campuses were very small. My message to the community was that portables were not a solution as the cost of portables and the cost of the site work needed made portables an economically poor choice.

Another plan was to build only a new high school and to place it on a relatively inexpensive site in a remote section of town. Because of the road system, this would have required Westborough to transport its high school students through two other towns to approach the new high school. Although I personally liked the idea of a new high school rather than a renovation expansion of our existing facility, without better access roads, this plan was problematic. Also, this solution did not adequately address overcrowding at the elementary school level. I already had spoken publicly against this proposal, when it had been presented at the prior town meeting.

I also continually communicated to the community the complete cost of the project based on the average household in Westborough. At least people could make their own decisions if the project were affordable. Each time I talked in the community, I communicated the fact that the state of Massachusetts would pay 55 percent of the construction costs of new or renovated schools. I acknowledged that times were tough, but there was no guarantee that if we waited, the state would be able to continue this type of funding. To delay could mean additional funding problems in the future.

Finally, I had a series of meetings with senior citizens. This group would be most affected by property tax increases as some of these people had become house rich but income poor. They had bought their houses many years ago, and now the houses were very valuable, which meant their property taxes had increased dramatically. Unfortunately, the seniors were on fixed incomes, and the additional taxes imposed a burden on them. I viewed this group as the greatest source of opposition.

To my amazement, the seniors proved easier to convince than I had anticipated. Their issue revolved more around the location of the school buildings. They were irritated by a prior proposal by a town study group to build a new high school on a remote site, which they viewed as inaccessible for senior citizens. "If we pay for it, we want to see it and use it," one senior commented to me. My message to these people was, "You approve the school, and I will be happy to recommend an addition/renovation project at our current downtown campus." The support of a large contingent of senior citizens prevented the building of a coalition against the school project.

I also met with parent groups, civic groups, teacher groups, realtors, and any group that would offer me the opportunity to communicate the message. Public forums were scheduled to explain all aspects of the project and to answer questions. If the project failed, it would not be due to lack of information.

Results

Ronald Reagan proved correct. The Soviet Union did soon crumble. One of the reasons was that the Soviets could not keep pace with President Reagan's aggressive military spending. With the demise of communism in the Soviet Union, other countries began to depart from communism. Shortly after President Reagan left office, the former Soviet satellites of Eastern Europe all overthrew their governments. In addition, Reagan's negotiations partner, Premier Mikhail Gorbachev, was toppled from his leadership position, and a new government came to power, which outlawed the communist party. The Soviet Union itself split into a group of independent countries.

As for Westborough, the voters at town meeting overwhelmingly approved $70 million for a renovation/expansion at the high school and a new elementary school. Interestingly enough, it was the senior citizens who voted overwhelmingly to support the schools.

Yes, both of these stories had happy endings. However, it is important to realize that as superintendent, no matter how well you connect with the public and regardless of how strong your message is, sometimes the ultimate decision may be made by the school board or by public vote. Still, no matter what the outcome, it is important that the superintendent exercise leadership through effective communication with the public and with staff.

Reflection Points

- Keep messages simple. People are busy and do not have the time or inclination to translate complex communications. When discussing educational issues in the community, remember that citizens want to hear why your recommended course of action is best for children.
- Be visible in the schools, at school events, and in the community. Visibility enhances credibility. Residents like to see their leaders, and visibility demonstrates commitment.
- Project optimism in conveying your message. People are by nature optimistic, and they respond well to leaders who are optimistic.
- Do not pretend that you always have the answer. The public admires humility and honesty. If you do not know an answer, it is far better to say so than to pretend that you do. You can always get back to people once you have done additional research on the topic.
- Even with your busy schedule, make communication a priority. The community will only support you if they know what you are doing. Remember that communication skills encompass two important components, connectivity and message.
- Don't personalize battles with your critics. Remain respectful and civil in spite of possible provocations from people who may not always be civil.
- Be a good listener as well as a good speaker. Listen carefully and then address thoughtfully issues that arise from the public.
- Work diligently to inform senior citizens about school issues. Seniors are often a vocal segment of the town that turn out disproportionately to their numbers to attend town meeting. Informed seniors will be knowledgeable voters who may become accepting of school initiatives. They, too, have a stake in education as a sound school system adds to the value of local real estate, contributes to town pride, and, in some cases, educates their grandchildren.

CHAPTER SEVEN

———— ❧ ————

Resolving School Board Issues

In Bohemia, there was once a method of deposing of government officials by throwing them out of windows. This technique was called defenestration. Although modern times are too sophisticated for this type of activity, the terminating of a superintendent who is unable to work with the school board can be almost as brutal as character and competency issues are often raised publicly. It is imperative for both educational effectiveness and personal survival that a superintendent learn to work cooperatively with the school board.

As an assistant superintendent, I learned about the dangers of school board/superintendent conflict by witnessing a modern-day defenestration of my one-time boss, former Westborough superintendent Jane Bottomley. The only thing lacking in this defenestration was an actual window and the ceremonial throw. All the other elements of the humiliation and pain of being stripped of power were present.

Ironically, the relationship between the school board and Jane had started off very well as she followed a very unpopular superintendent. After an initial honeymoon period, which most superintendents usually receive, the relationship quickly broke down. During school board meetings, there would be continuing bickering between the superintendent and the committee members concerning the responsibilities of

101

each. Jane would claim that the committee was micromanaging her, while the committee felt that Jane was continually ignoring their suggestions. The night of the actual defenestration was particularly tense. During that school board meeting, three members of the committee were arguing with the superintendent over some minor procedures for graduation. Suddenly, heated words began to be exchanged between Jane and the members of the committee. The room suddenly became silent. The superintendent and the school board chair began glaring at each other. Finally, Superintendent Bottomley clumsily tried to bring the issue to an end.

"Let's forget politics and do what is right for the kids. My plan is a good one, which I know will work, and I am your superintendent," she stressed.

"Not for long," responded the school board chair in an ominous tone.

This conflict was making me quite uncomfortable.

"I move we go into executive session," said the school board chair a few seconds later.

This confrontation was getting unpleasant. Jane turned to me and said, "Whatever you do, stick with me in executive session."

The chair turned to me and said, "Good night, Stephen."

I responded, "I prefer to stay."

The chair repeated, "Good night, Stephen."

I looked her right in the eye and said, "Good night." I consider myself a loyal person, but I'm not foolish. At that point, I realized that there was nothing I could do to remedy the problem. We were about to lose our superintendent in Westborough.

Jane had lost the confidence and support of the school board, which is usually synonymous with losing one's job. Minimally, a superintendent must work cooperatively with the school board to make the school system work. School boards, whether elected or appointed, are the representatives of the people. A superintendent cannot ignore making them a part of the process. However, that is exactly what happened with Jane Bottomley.

How did she lose the committee? Some of it had to do with her management philosophy. She told me repeatedly, "The idea is to flood the school board with information to such an extent that they cannot possibly absorb it. You can then do what you want." This is probably the worst management advice I have ever received. School boards insist on being part of the educational process. They view themselves as decision makers and not just cheerleaders for the superintendent.

Jane did many wonderful things as superintendent. She was very knowledgeable about curriculum and developed an extensive curriculum-review process, which proved very useful to the school system. She was also a prodigious worker who would stay late into the evening, meeting with people and reviewing issues. Her biggest problem was that she forgot that the role of the superintendent is to work cooperatively with the school board. Too often, school board meetings became the Jane Bottomley show. Jane would make lengthy reports and then publicly stress the direction that she wished the school board to take. There was little real input from committee members.

The school board began resenting the passive role to which they were assigned. They then began looking for little things to embarrass Jane. The committee blasted her for purchasing "new outrageously expensive" office furniture when the year before, as an assistant, she had bought new office furniture. To the committee, this type of purchase showed her disregard for the financial needs of the system and was one more example of Jane putting her wants above the needs of the students. School board meetings became increasingly adversarial, and executive sessions would run late into the evening with the room cleared except for the superintendent and the committee. Following these sessions, I could see Jane was visibly shaken. No one was surprised when she was advised by the committee to pursue another position.

Jane Bottomley was not the only area superintendent to be released due to issues with the school board. In a neighboring town, a superintendent of schools made front-page news by paying $2,000 with district funds for a ticket to California to attend the superintendent's convention instead of the standard fare of $400. His reason was that the ticket could be cancelled at any time without penalty, and if a problem arose in the district, he could cancel and receive a full refund. This logic made no sense to the school board. Consequently, his committee gave him a one-way ticket out of town. Another superintendent had his contract terminated because he plagiarized a graduation speech. Even after a formal apology, the committee made him persona non grata. In all of these cases, the actual events were probably not the primary reason for termination. What happened was that the school board had lost confidence in the superintendent because of the superintendent's inability to work with the school board. So, what is the secret to being successful as a superintendent?

Working cooperatively with the school board is certainly a good starting point. Remember, the school board is your supervisor. The committee represents the community, and they should never be ignored or patronized. The superintendency is a partnership with these people, and they do not wish to be silent partners. They did not run for office to become yes men and women for you. Rather, they are civic-minded people who run for the school board for many different reasons. As superintendent, it is imperative that you value their input and work with the members of the school board.

You should, however, never compromise your professionalism as this quality is a necessity for success as a superintendent. Remember, just as a superintendent needs the school board, the school board needs the superintendent. We have the expertise and the experience to deal with the complex issues that regularly face the school system. We do this on a daily basis, and that is what helps make the school system successful. School boards do want a capable decision maker in charge as the committee is legitimately concerned about the welfare of the students. No school board enjoys seeing the system flounder due to poor leadership. We also provide the school board with the information needed to make good decisions. Committee members rely on us to provide them with extensive backup material for their public discussions and well-thought-out recommendations.

School board members want their input heard. Still, this does not mean you should ignore your own standards by merely doing it their way. A superintendent must recommend to the school board what he believes is best for the children. Sometimes, when I'm at odds with a committee member, that member may say, "Steve I totally disagree." I merely smile and say, "Disagreement is fine, and reasonable people can disagree. However, you asked me what I recommend, and this is what I recommend." Being honest and straightforward about what you stand for is to be respected. At the same time, being flexible enough to work with the committee if they choose to go in a different direction is equally important. Understanding the politics of the role of superintendent is imperative.

In addition to working with the committee as a whole, the superintendent must address differences between individual members in order to keep the committee functioning effectively. Splits in the committee create hard feeling and can make the school board less functional.

In Westborough, we had one school board member publicly oppose the reelection of another school board member. After the election, I had to work with both members to reconcile their differences. The worst situation I witnessed was where the chair of the school board spoke to me about a member whom she alleged had spoken critically in public about decisions of the school board. She asked for a meeting with me and that member in my office to discuss the conflict. The approach sounded reasonable to me as I like to talk out differences to resolve problems. I arranged the meeting as requested. As soon as the meeting began, the chair began berating the other member. She screamed in her face about how she was a disgrace to the committee. She accused this member of being disloyal and hypocritical and approached her with the same intensity as a batter confronting an umpire over a controversial called third strike. As I had never encountered a situation like this, I watched in amazement. The chair then turned on me and said angrily, "Are you going to join in or are you just another pretty face." The meeting was now spinning out of control. At that point, I tried to restore calm as the other member was emotionally upset.

As superintendents, we work in situations charged with emotion, but it is imperative that we superintendents strive to keep members from becoming disrespectful to each other. A battle between committee members is a no-win situation for us. It is important to attempt to resolve these internal conflicts in a peaceful manner as soon and as amicably as possible.

To be successful, a superintendent must also be able to work with the diverse concerns of the school board, as well as the demands of the teachers, parents, and community. As the system moves forward, how does the superintendent keep people together in a constructive way?

George H. W. Bush in the Gulf War serves as a model for keeping a diverse coalition together.

Defining the Problem

President Bush was confronted with a major foreign policy problem when on August 2, 1990, an Iraqi army of one hundred thousand men invaded and then occupied Kuwait. Not only did this action jeopardize the safety of the people of Kuwait, but it also threatened a large source of the world's oil supply. Now that Kuwait was occupied, was an invasion of our ally, oil-rich Saudi Arabia, imminent?

Some type of military engagement between Iraq and Kuwait did not come as a surprise to the world. Saddam Hussein, the president of Iraq, had been speaking aggressively for some months concerning his proposed grievances against the Kuwaiti government. Hussein was angered over what he viewed as Kuwait's overbearing attitude over loans that Iraq needed to pay back to Kuwait for its financial assistance in Iraq's 1980–1988 war against Iran. Hussein also accused Kuwait of overproducing in its wells, which kept oil prices down and further hurt the Iraqi economy. However, an outright invasion and occupation was more than anticipated. Hussein justified the invasion by asserting that, historically, Kuwait had been a part of Iraq before the land was divided by the colonial powers. According to Hussein, the invasion would correct a wrong that had been done to his country.

President George Bush made it clear from the outset that he would not tolerate this act of aggression. Still, action against Iraq would be a departure from our former position in the region. The United States had previously been supportive of Iraq, for many Americans saw Iraq as a counterweight to the religious fundamentalism that threatened the region. America had also supplied Hussein with military aid during the Iran-Iraq war in which Iraq was only able to succeed due to American help. As much as many people would question Hussein's oppression of people in his own country, compared to the mullahs of Iran, he was perceived as a cornerstone of stability in the Middle East.

Given our previous history of support for Iraq, the lack of American forces in the region, and the unwillingness of Saddam Hussein to withdraw voluntarily without concessions, how would President Bush be able to evict the Iraqi forces from Kuwait?

In Westborough, my problem also arose quickly, and somewhat unexpectedly, during what I thought was going to be an uneventful school board meeting. As with the Iraqi invasion, there had been some warnings in advance. On two previous occasions, parents had come to the school board concerned about teachers whom they felt treated their children in a callous and mean-spirited manner during extracurricular activities. They approached the school board because they believed that they had received no satisfaction from the building principal or me. In each case, I had reminded the school board that because there were two sides to each story, the teachers could not be presumed guilty as there was also testimony to the contrary. In addition, as these were personnel matters, I could not legally discuss publicly the disciplinary actions taken by the principals. I mistakenly thought the matter was settled. In the spring, a mother came forward to complain about a classroom teacher, and I knew that this complaint would be more problematic because she brought with her the wife of a school board member. The parent complained about a teacher who already had a reputation for being extremely insensitive to children. I could see that the school board was very supportive of this parent, and I could understand why. Parents for years had complained about this teacher's berating their children. Still, it would be inappropriate for me as superintendent to describe publicly the actions taken by the principal with this teacher. I knew this was going to mushroom into a larger problem when two members of the school board stated, during the meeting, that bullying was a major issue in our schools, and they, too, had children who were bullied by teachers in their classrooms. The issue was accelerating. The newspapers began to write about bullying as a problem in the Westborough Public Schools. Now the question was, How was I going to handle this contentious issue as superintendent?

Putting the Issue into Perspective

As H. L. Mencken once wrote, "There is always a well-known solution to every human problem—neat, plausible and wrong." The public can always suggest a solution. Sometimes that solution will solve the problem but at the same time create other more serious systemwide issues. People tend to look at issues through the viewpoint of how the issue affects them. A leader has to look at the broad picture and make a decision that is best for the entire system.

George Bush knew that the United States had the resources to easily win a military confrontation with Saddam Hussein. However, there were many factors complicating the issue. It is not enough to merely solve a problem if you create a greater problem.

President Bush had many factors to consider. First, Iraq was a long way from the United States in an area where America did not have military bases from which to launch an assault on the Iraqi troops in Kuwait. Air bases would have to be established in the Middle East in order to strike at Iraq. Military bases would also have to be constructed in the area to deploy our ground troops, who would actually wage combat with the Iraqi Army. This would not be easy as American relations with the countries in the region were sometimes strained because of American support for the state of Israel. To many who lived in the Arab states, Israel only existed because of American military support for the Jewish state. The Palestinians and the Jordanians were particularly outspoken about the need for Arabs to solve their own problems without the intervention of the United States or other Western countries.

The other large Arab states, which included Egypt, Syria, and Saudi Arabia, also had fears of active American involvement in the region. Each country had a large population of fundamentalist Muslims who hated Westerners and feared Western influences coming into the area. The idea of stationing Western troops in an Arab country such as Saudi Arabia would be a radical departure from their tradition.

Saddam Hussein was quick to exploit anti-Israeli feelings among the Arabs in an attempt to win support for his aggression. He would tell Arab countries that he was quite willing to leave Kuwait if the United States would force Israel to settle their issues with the Palestinians. Hussein also argued that Iraq was an Arab partner, while the United States was a colonial power who only cared about the oil in the region and who was no friend of the Arabs. This approach won support with many fundamentalist Arabs in the area. Hussein even went so far as to attempt to buy the support of key Arab countries through the promise of sharing the revenues from the Kuwaiti oil with them. Israel was a problem. If the United States were to get support in the area, Israel would have to have no part in any united effort to fight Saddam Hussein. The Arab states would never join the United States in any military action that involved their hated enemy. The problem was that Israeli leaders also heard the threats of Saddam Hussein to incinerate their country. They would be reluctant not to retaliate against any aggression as they felt it would show weakness to a hated enemy. In spite of a long-standing friendship with Israel, President George Bush knew that he would have to keep Israel on the sidelines in any fighting if he was going to work jointly with Arab states.

Many countries throughout the world were uneasy about joining a coalition with the United States for a potential military campaign against Saddam Hussein. These countries had their own domestic issues, which appeared to be a far higher priority than engaging in a military campaign in a highly volatile region of the world. Some, such as the Soviet Union, were trading partners with Iraq and did not wish to disrupt this relationship.

Finally, even in this country, many Americans did not want to see military action in the Persian Gulf region. Americans felt lingering disillusionment from the Vietnam experience and still mourned the large number of American casualties. They did not want America engaged militarily in a long-term conflict in the desert. Many Americans were reluctant to spend billions of dollars to station American forces halfway around the world for an indefinite amount of time. A large military response against Iraq might not be an easy sell domestically.

Like George Bush, I attempted to anticipate the issues I would face in resolving the issue. Certainly, the school board was demanding immediate action. Its members had shown sympathy to the parents concerned about bullying teachers, and they wanted to demonstrate their power to address the issue in a timely manner. Certainly, an issue about a teacher's being mean to children gets school board members and parents emotionally angry, and I knew I would have to do something immediately to address the issue. Superintendents are often lightning rods for the school board's frustrations. I felt, by the tone of their voices and the pointedness of their questions, that perhaps I was headed for my own defenestration.

There was also anger from the other direction. Many teachers were outraged by the position of the school board. Some teachers spoke to me of their ire at being portrayed as bullies. They believed that if parents perceived them as bullies, they could not be as effective. "If I keep a student after school because he disrupts the class, am I a bully?" one teacher asked. "How about parents bullying us?" asked another indignant teacher. Several teachers expressed frustration that the parent complainer did not even meet first with the teacher before going to the administration and the school board.

The teachers' association would not prove helpful. Its executive committee believed that even acknowledging it added legitimacy to the complaint of teachers as bullies. The teachers' association circulated a letter stating that no teachers should sign up for any committee that addressed the issue of bullying. They believed the parent was wrong in the matter, and the administration and school board should not look for any type of political compromise to solve the problem. This us-versus-them, parent-versus-teacher perspective would only compound the difficulty. I was looking for solutions to diffuse a difficult public situation and was not looking to exacerbate the existing problem. Still, I did want to find a way to work with the teachers' union to address the issue of bullying.

Parents were also weighing in on this topic with both me and the school board. To some, it was time the school board and the administration addressed the issue of poor teachers. "How many complaints about a teacher are needed before appropriate action is taken?" asked one parent at a public meeting. Several people had encountered problems with this same teacher over the years, and these people felt little had been done by the administration to rectify the situation. They sympathized with the parents who had brought the issue to the school board. To these parents, setting guidelines to protect the students from the arbitrary conduct of teachers was a reasonable solution. I did not meet anyone who said, "The teachers are a bunch of bullies." Rather, parents would talk about the few "bad teachers" who needed to be addressed by the administration.

Community reaction was mixed. Some people applauded parents' finally standing up to the school board and the superintendent to make sure students were protected. Others said the yuppies were just trying to spoil their kids and to blame the teachers for the failings of their own children. "Hey, in life you have to learn how to live with people you don't particularly like, so students should work out their problems with the teachers," reasoned a senior citizen who spoke with me outside my office. In all cases, community members wanted "bad teachers" disciplined.

Regardless of who is right or wrong, when a problem gets to the school board level, there is no question who owns the problem. As superintendent, you own all, or at least a major portion of, public educational issues. As one member of my school board constantly reminded me, "You are the most highly paid public problem solver in this community." Now that I had put the problem into perspective, what could be done about it?

Planning and Executing

President George Bush took time to frame the issue in a way that would promote success. Instead of this being a conflict between the United States and Iraq, the issue he constructed was Saddam Hussein versus the world. His plan was to forge a coalition to drive Hussein from Kuwait.

After the invasion of Kuwait, world support for Hussein was minimal, so Bush had fertile ground on which to work. Most countries believed Iraqi aggression against Kuwait in the oil-rich area would cause further problems in this volatile region. President Bush had little trouble working with the United Nations Security Council, which quickly voted for economic sanctions against Iraq.

Sanctions were one thing, but getting nations to agree to military intervention was another. To develop a coalition of nations to force Saddam Hussein to withdraw from Kuwait became the highest priority of the Bush administration. President Bush's efforts were tireless as he made phone calls and met with world leaders regularly to forge an alliance. He made James Baker, the secretary of state, a roving ambassador to ensure communication was effective so that each leader felt like a valued member of the alliance. For any leader, communication is the key to any successful joint venture.

Increasingly, world leaders became outraged against Hussein because of the wide number of atrocities committed by his troops in Kuwait and because of his attempt to use foreign nationals as human shields around Iraqi military installations. These actions would allow George Bush to further frame the debate as a question of good versus evil, and it would be difficult for any nation to ignore what Iraq was doing during its occupation of Kuwait.

The Arab countries committed to joining a coalition far more quickly than originally anticipated. The Saudi's were particularly nervous about the intentions of Hussein's army, which was stationed not far from their border. They did agree to put American bases on their soil, where the coalition would later launch its attack against Iraq. Saudi Arabia was also concerned about being the only Arab state to commit. Egypt entered the coalition at the behest of President Bush, who offered to forgive the Egyptian debt to the United States, which ran into the billions of dollars. Even Syria helped by convincing Iran not to get involved with helping Hussein as he was a man who could not be trusted. Israel's willingness to refrain from retaliating, even when attacked by Scud missiles from Iraq, served to solidify the alliance and to make the Arab participants in the coalition even more comfortable.

Led by Britain, many other countries worldwide began to join the military alliance. President Bush was wise enough to allow them time to convince their own citizens of the need for action as others were convinced that the last thing that their country needed was involvement in a Middle East war. Even Soviet president Mikhail Gorbachev agreed that if Hussein would not voluntarily withdraw his troops from Kuwait, the Iraqi military would have to be forced out. Over thirty nations would eventually join the coalition against Iraq. President George Bush was committed to solving the problem through an international effort.

With no signs of a movement toward Iraqi withdrawal, world leaders became increasingly committed to evicting Iraq from Kuwait. The United Nations Security Council passed a resolution that Hussein would have to leave within forty-five days or the coalition could take "all necessary means" to evict the Iraqi forces. George Bush patiently waited for the time line to elapse. To assure both international and domestic critics that he was trying to use diplomacy to prevent war, Bush sent his secretary of state to tell Hussein to withdraw his forces from Kuwait or have them forcefully evicted. Even this threat did not influence the Iraqi leader. On January 15, the time line expired, and the coalition went to war to drive Iraqi troops from Kuwait.

In Westborough, given that there were so many special-interest groups on this issue, as President Bush did, I wanted to forge a coalition. As superintendent, it is a lot easier to develop a solution when you have the support of the interested parties. A committee was formed with representatives from the school board, administration, parents, and teachers to review the issue. Now it appeared progress could be made.

Like Bush, I wanted first to frame the issues. Although the school board had made it clear that it wanted a bullying policy that addressed the teacher issue, I believed that they would accept the latitude of a broader review. A committee concerned with teacher bullying would serve only to continue to antagonize teachers and not really address the issue of bullying within the school system. It was time to look at the larger problem.

Since the Westborough school community was composed of staff, children, and parents, why not develop a policy that addressed respect among all members of the system? Yes, there were some issues with teachers that had to be addressed. However, there were also occasional conflicts between overbearing parents and teachers, which could not be ignored. Certainly, the biggest problem of bullying within our system was student-to-student, and this issue had to be reviewed. At my urging, the committee voted to name itself the "mutual respect committee" rather than "the committee on bullying." The committee members agreed that our stated mission should be to develop a policy that clearly prohibited "bullying among all members of the school community." Who could disagree with this?

I found out quickly. There are problems with keeping any coalition together, and Westborough proved no exception. Although three teachers volunteered to serve on the committee, two withdrew for "personal reasons." I knew they were getting pressure from other teachers concerning their willingness to serve. I called the third teacher into my office and gave her the opportunity to resign from the committee rather than be the only teacher in the entire system to consent to work with administration on the bullying issue. She did resign and appreciated my understanding. To me it was a matter of keeping that teacher's dignity by not singling her out to the staff as a perceived ally of the administration. Anyway, it would not really help to say there was teacher input if we only had one token teacher. In any event, one volunteer teacher could not adequately represent four hundred teachers, and to try do so, I believed, would make a mockery of the system.

Luckily, I did convince the president of the union to attend the meetings of the Mutual Respect Committee, which was a better alternative. I advised her that if she attended, even without formally joining the committee, at least she could hear what was said, and she could respond accordingly. She and the union's executive committee would eventually come up with twenty recommendations for the policy. This was helpful as it provided needed and legitimate teacher input. This proved to be a more effective method for staff buy-in than I anticipated.

There were also issues among the parents. The three parents who waged complaints were disappointed that they had not been appointed to the committee. They felt excluded and believed the committee might not address their issues. Although I do try to include diverse opinions in committees, I feared that these parents, who were actually quite nice, were so emotionally involved that they might lose focus as to the mission of the committee and continue to be concerned only with their own individual cases. The parents who served on the committee were objective and quite reasonable throughout the process. None of them was looking for a draconian code; rather, they wanted to solve the problem.

The committee researched other similar policies and found some in Connecticut and others in Canada. We sent for copies, and they proved quite helpful. I did speak to the superintendents who had sent along their policies personally to show my commitment. Their policies helped the committee to produce a document in four months that defined bullying and specified the penalties for violations. Bullying was defined by our committee as, "repeated acts which ridicule, humiliate, or intimidate another person." In matrix fashion, the committee designed a punishment grid based on the number and severity of offenses. The committee had done its job.

Results

The coalition forces quickly defeated the army of Saddam Hussein. In fact, after the bombing from the air was completed, it took only one hundred hours of ground action by coalition troops for the president to declare victory and call a halt to hostilities. There were over a half-million dead or wounded Iraqis, and their country was devastated. There were major problems in Iraq with lack of water, sewer, electricity, food, and other necessities. To continue the war, the president reasoned, would only serve to trample a defeated foe and create a legacy of anti-American feeling in the area. The president also did not want to push forward to drive Saddam Hussein from power and occupy Iraq out of fear that the coalition would dissolve if the original mission of the campaign was changed. President Bush felt that he had solved the problem by driving the Iraqis out of Kuwait.

Twelve years later, his son George W. Bush would again go to war against the forces of Saddam Hussein with a second coalition. Hussein would be defeated and captured. America currently occupies Iraq, and only time will reveal the success of this initiative.

In Westborough, the school board unanimously approved the recommended policy of the Mutual Respect Committee. During that school board meeting, the Mutual Respect Committee spokesman, who was a parent, emphasized that the policy "would not in any way undermine the authority of the teachers and staff to effectively discipline students and enforce school and classroom rules." All groups appeared satisfied. Following this report, the issue appeared to disappear as parents now had a mechanism in place to address the issue if needed. Ah, one problem solved; only about five thousand more issues needed to be addressed during that school year.

Reflection Points

- Treat the school board as a partner in the process of education. Communicate regularly by phone with the members of the committee. They like hearing from you, and communication will prevent surprises during public meetings.

- Be a good listener. Members of the committee like to be heard. Their input is important.
- You should have an idea of the outcome of school board agenda items before the meeting. Discussion with the school board prior to the meeting can give you a sense of the direction the meeting will take. It can also serve to clarify the issues and to avoid confusion when these issues are brought forward during the meeting.
- Do not give the school board the impression that you believe the issues are too complex for them to understand. Your job is to make the issues understandable. Brief summaries, support material, and your recommendations should be sent to the school board, along with other materials in advance of the meeting.
- In making recommendations to the committee, do not stray from your own belief system. Give them your best advice, knowing they might move in another direction.
- Do not personalize disagreements with the school board. The issue should always focus on what is best for the students. Do not allow ego to affect your relationship with the school board.

CHAPTER EIGHT

Budget

"It was the best of times, it was the worst of times." Charles Dickens introduced his novel *A Tale of Two Cities* with these memorable words. This description could also apply to the budget process for a superintendent. In the best of times, you win approval for a financial plan, which provides the resources to develop and to expand opportunities for children. During the worst of times, your budget is defeated, and you have to retrench and attempt to maintain the quality programs that you already have. In either case, the budgeting process is a challenging, time-consuming, and often nerve-wracking part of your job.

Compiling a school budget is relatively simple. It takes a basic knowledge of seventh-grade mathematics, a devotion to detail, and the ability to use a spreadsheet. However, creating a budget that best addresses the needs of the students in a school system and can garner the support of the community is an arduous task. With limited resources, we as superintendents must exercise sound judgment in making financial decisions, then have the courage to defend those choices.

Like most superintendents, I do not see myself as a number cruncher. Most of us began our careers teaching an academic discipline, other than math, at the secondary level or several disciplines at the elementary school level. We were promoted to management positions, and as

117

it does for any new manager, budgeting became crucial. When we became superintendents, sound financial management became an even higher priority. At a recent superintendents' meeting, one experienced superintendent stated a commonly held view of the importance of closely monitoring school finances: "Mismanaging the budget can get you fired. A school board will forgive you for an unsuccessful reading or math program, but mismanaging public funds usually means termination." Although this is an oversimplification of the complex relationship between the school board and superintendent, I would agree that sound financial management is important to the survival of a superintendent. Errors involving town funds become public knowledge quickly and often cause the school board and the community to lose faith in the superintendent's ability to properly administer the school system.

Fortunately, like many chief executive officers, we often have assistance in budget preparation and management. These support people are frequently named business managers, administrative assistants, or assistant superintendents for business. At Westborough, I was fortunate to have a highly competent assistant superintendent who was extremely capable in the area of finance. He had an MBA, and he was comfortable discussing budget numbers and making quick financial adjustments as needed. The joke among the school board members was that when I said I was running the numbers, that meant I was running them down the hall for my assistant to analyze. Still, although subordinates can be very helpful with financial matters, the primary responsibility lies with the superintendent, and a large amount of our time must be devoted to this task.

Sometimes a superintendent can be tripped up by financial circumstances over which he or she has very little control. Several years ago, Jim Gray, a friend of mine, took over a small superintendency in a nearby town. One day, he told his secretary that he was going to a meeting with the principals in the district, and he did not want to be disturbed unless it was an emergency. Thirty minutes into the meeting, the phone rang. It was his secretary. Jim was somewhat agitated and snapped at her, "What can be so important that it can't wait for another ninety minutes?" She calmly explained, "The police have just handcuffed the business manner, and he is being driven away in a cruiser." The business manager for years had set up dummy companies and had the school department pay bogus bills to these companies. This individual was eventually sentenced to prison for fifteen years. My friend Jim was advised by the school board to find another position. Although Jim had only been at his post for a year and a half, the school board told him the theft was done on his watch, and he was therefore negligent. The fact that the fraud had transpired for six years prior to his arrival had little effect on the school board's decision. When there is a problem with the budget, you as superintendent are responsible.

The budget process in Westborough is similar to the procedure in all Massachusetts cities and towns. It often begins with the teachers working in departments or in grade-level teams making requests that are reviewed by their principal. The principal then adds or deletes items as he sees fit and forwards the building budget to the superintendent. The superintendent then makes necessary adjustments to the principals' budgets, adds in systemwide needs, such as transportation and utility costs, and submits a recommended school-district budget to the school board. Over a six-week period, the school board reviews the budget publicly, then either approves the superintendent's recommendation or approves an adjusted figure. The most difficult part of the process is the public engagement. School board meetings are televised, and there are reporters and town residents in the audience. As the school board rightly wants to show due diligence to the community, the principals and I are closely questioned about the necessity for each request. My proposed budget is usually lowered at the completion of school board review. The next step is for me and the school board to meet publicly with the town finance committee for a budget review. The finance committee is charged with making a recommendation to the Westborough town meeting. The town meeting vote ultimately determines the actual budget.

Even with school board reductions to the budget, problems loom ahead with the finance committee. In Massachusetts, the finance committee is the financial watchdog of community monies. Members perceive their job to be to ensure that the town finances are solid, and they scrutinize the budgets of all town departments looking for what they call "fat." The meeting with the finance committee usually requires a number of hours, with topics ranging from the percentage of the total town budget comprised by the school-system budget to why the budget should not be reduced. They often become frustrated with the complexity of uncontrollable factors, such as state aid, special education costs, and increases in fixed costs.

As with the school board, I make every effort to be patient and courteous with finance committee members. After all, these people have a difficult job to do, and they do serve many hours without any financial compensation. One criticism that does make me bristle at these meeting is the comment, "The schools should run more like a business." I've never understood the meaning of that criticism. Schools are different from businesses, I patiently explain. Businesses are able to divest themselves of programs that do not work or are too expensive to maintain. However, schools cannot, nor should they, divest themselves of expensive programs such as special education or English-language-learner programs. Business also has greater flexibility than schools. Businesses can cut costs by relocating to other areas of the country or to other areas of the world. I joke with the finance committee members, saying that it might be difficult to explain to parents that I have decided to outsource the whole system to Sri Lanka in order to reduce costs. Also, as mentioned earlier, business's primary concern is market share. In schools, we work to satisfy all customers as even one angry parent can create a political firestorm.

I know that even before our presentation on the budget to the finance committee, we will hear, "This is a tough year financially for Westborough." It is the same greeting we have received in all my seventeen years in the town.

I try not to become perturbed when the questions stray off the subject of budget. "Why don't you do something about the teenagers spray-painting stop signs in town?" I patiently explain that we do not often know if these children were Westborough students or not, and certainly we do not punish the innocent. "How about putting a suggestion box in each school so the teachers can confidentially put down their ideas for reducing expenditures? In one school I've heard that one of the principals does not allow the faculty any meaningful input into the school budget." Although I was comfortable with the existing process to solicit teacher input, I did, to placate the finance committee, send the faculty a letter saying they could write to me anonymously if they had suggestions on better controlling the budget. I was not surprised when I received about thirty letters, all of which stated a need to raise, not reduce, the budget. Teachers suggested restoration of classroom aids, a reduction in class size, and increased funding for materials. At finance committee and at all public budget meetings, I emphasize the importance of quality education rather than just talking numbers. I am not as fast at calculating numbers as the members of the finance committee, and I don't pretend to be. However, the members of the finance committee do often get excited hearing about the new programs in the school department. After all, learning about innovative educational programs that serve children is inherently more interesting to them than hearing about the Department of Public Works' need to increase the budget for salt and sand to treat the town's roads during inclement weather or the fire department's need to overhaul one of its fire engines.

During one particular year that went exceptionally well with the finance committee, I explained at length how the school was budgeting $40,000 to engage in a virtual high school whereby we would partner with forty other schools from all over the world to allow our students to take courses over the Internet. This project excited the members of the finance committee and stimulated a vibrant discussion. They wholeheartedly approved of the program and appeared to become somewhat friendlier about their budget questions. When I meet with the finance committee, I stress education rather than merely talking about the need to keep pace with inflation. The discussion is framed, as much as possible, around how the budget enhances learning opportunities for students. The argument that we need an increase to just maintain service does not sell well to a budget review board. We as superintendents must convince people that the money is needed to benefit students and that the money will be well spent.

About six weeks after meeting with the finance committee, the school board and I present the budget at town meeting. No matter how many years I have been a school administrator, I am nervous going into town meeting. In Westborough, all voters are eligible to attend town meeting, so I am never sure of the composition of the audience. People are free to ask whatever question they like concerning the budget. The tone of some of the questions can be extremely hostile, with people demanding to know why we cannot curtail school department spending. As a former history teacher, to me, town meeting has all the elements of the medieval practice of trial by fire. Like the accused in the Middle Ages who was made to carry a red-hot iron bar for nine paces to prove his innocence, I must face the red-hot anger of disgruntled members of the public. The argument against the budget usually is that the school department spends extravagantly. From the tone of the comments, it sounds like I, as superintendent, am working diligently for strategies to drive out the poor, the sick, and indigent from the borders of the town. I do understand that the local taxes are oppressive to senior citizens and to people of limited means. However, I have to be concerned about children. I view myself as the champion of children when I am advocating for sufficient funds to support programs to best educate the youth of Westborough in order to prepare them for a better future. I never apologize for the budget. My view is that if I do not stand up for the quality of a Westborough education, then who will. I view myself as a leader when I defend the school budget at town meeting. President Bill Clinton demonstrated this same type of leadership commitment in his struggle with congressional Republicans in developing the FY 96 federal budget.

The Challenge

President Clinton had entered the budget debate in a weakened position due to intense public criticism over his failed attempt to get Congress to approve one of his highest priorities, universal health care. He had also antagonized many people by raising taxes on the top 2 percent of American taxpayers. Raising taxes is a politically charged issue for any president. Although taxing the wealthy may appear to be a popular national issue, many people are concerned about the possibility that tax increases may begin with the wealthy but later extend to them. There is also a concern on the part of some people that they will someday become wealthy, and they will have to pay these higher taxes.

In addition, there had been serious issues raised about Clinton's character following revelations of alleged financial improprieties concerning Whitewater, a real estate transaction in Arkansas in which he had invested while serving as governor, and allegations of sexual misconduct with a state employee while he was governor. The time was ripe for a congressional challenge to the power of the presidency.

Representative Newt Gingrich, a congressman who would later become the speaker of the House of Representatives, became the spokesperson for this challenge. Gingrich had been a longtime advocate of greater congressional power, and the fall elections of 1994 appeared the ideal opportunity to confront the president in a move to transfer greater power to Congress. Gingrich saw these upcoming elections as a chance to assert his own leadership and to make the elections a national referendum on the direction of the country.

The differences between the congressman and the president were clear. President Clinton perceived the federal government as an effective vehicle to solve the problems of Americans, while Representative Gingrich and his allies saw government as becoming too large, wasteful, and a burden to the American taxpayer. They believed the state governments could take over many responsibilities of the federal government and deliver these services more efficiently. The federal budget would later become the focus of the debate.

In the fall of 1994, Newt Gingrich gathered three hundred Republicans, who were either members of the House of Representatives or candidates for election to the House, on the steps of the Capitol and issued their "Contract with America." This program, he emphasized, was designed to streamline government and make it more responsive to the American people. Gingrich went even further by telling the public, "If we break this contract, throw us out. We mean it." The contract proved a public relations success. People liked the contract and what they perceived as the high level of accountability.

During the election campaign, Newt Gingrich campaigned strongly against President Clinton and urged Americans to vote against the Democrats. He called the president and his wife, Hillary, "counterculture McGovernicks" and referred to the president himself as "the enemy of normal people." The Republicans convincingly won a majority of the congressional elections of 1994, and the stage was set to challenge the president's economic program.

As superintendents of schools, we have our own set of obstacles in getting a budget approved. In my own particular case, the fiscal year 2005 budget would present the most serious challenge to my leadership.

Westborough had never had any serious controversy concerning its school budget. The town had a large business base, which paid almost 40 percent of all property taxes to the town. The business tax revenue served as a financial shock absorber for the town as it kept the home owners' property taxes quite reasonable. However, there were warning signs that conditions were changing. As Westborough became an increasingly desirable town in which to live, property values skyrocketed, and the demand for town services also increased. This resulted in larger tax bills, which caused complaints by the residents, including many of our school supporters. For the first time, I began hearing, "The tax bills in this town are staggering. Can't the school department do anything to control spending?"

With the downturn in the Massachusetts economy, some Westborough residents began losing jobs, while others saw smaller raises, no raises, or wage declines. The complaints about school spending became louder. Other people were joining the demand for some type of tax relief and better control of school spending. In Westborough, school expenditures absorbed approximately 55 percent of the total town budget.

The real challenge was to explain to residents how, in spite of high taxes, there would not be adequate funding to support the schools unless there was another large local property tax increase. "We were fine the last two years. What happened to all the money?" I was asked at public meetings. The answer was simple, but it satisfied few people. In public finance, sometimes emotion triumphs over logic as people become frustrated over what they feel they cannot control.

I explained that a declining economy meant less aid from the state. For Westborough, this translated into a decrease of almost $1 million. At the local level, the town administrator projected a decrease of local receipts of $1 million due to such problems as fewer building permits and fewer hotel receipts, again because of the slowing economy. Compounding the difficulty of decreasing revenue was the spiraling increase of fixed expenses such as utilities, insurance, transportation, and out-of-district special education outside costs. Town insurance bills alone were going up almost $1 million annually due to soaring health insurance premiums. In the minds of many citizens, school department spending was to blame for increasing taxes. To compound the difficulty, the town would also have to begin debt and interest payments for a newly expanded/renovated high school and a new elementary school, which would add an additional $3 million expense for the town to fund.

As I was drafting a budget for school board approval, I could hear the mounting criticism:

- The police and fire departments can control spending, why can't the school department?
- Why do we have to try to be like Wayland? (Wayland is a wealthy town to the east of Westborough.)
- The yuppies are trying to take over the town and drive the rest of us out of here.

Then, the first organized challenge appeared. Its spokesman was a gentleman named Mike Davis, who had only recently moved into Westborough but who had been extremely active as leader of a group opposed to raising taxes in the nearby town in which he had lived previously. How many people he actually spoke for, we had no way of knowing. It could have been just himself or any number of school-spending critics. Mike Davis would periodically issue newsletters that stressed to the community that the school department spending was excessive. I did have to acknowledge the excellent charts and graphs he provided in his position papers. The facts were always accurate as he would constantly check his figures against those of the school department. However, his interpretation was certainly antischool:

- Taxes in Westborough up 49 percent in five years
- School salaries up 33 percent in six years
- Benefits to school employees up 102 percent in six years
- Teacher pay raises undeserved
- Union protective of poor teachers
- School system underperforming

How do you respond to this type of criticism without sounding defensive? Certainly, taxes were up due to the town's willingness to vote to support quality services in spite of decreases in state aid. Still, the message of the need to control spiraling costs, no matter what the reason, resonates well with the taxpayers. The controversy concerning school spending would not go away easily. My challenge was to prepare a budget that would be sellable to the community and meet the needs of the school system.

Strategy

President Clinton knew, from the outset, that he was in for a major confrontation over the budget. The Senate and the House of Representatives were now dominated by Republican majorities. Many of the newly elected representatives had won their elections by campaigning to support the Contract with America. They, therefore, would insist on a budget that conformed to these guidelines for fiscal austerity. Representative Newt Gingrich was already talking about a Republican revolution, which would downsize government and cut taxes. The task for President Bill Clinton was to rebuff the challenge by developing a budget that would win the support of the American people.

As President Clinton had the advantage of continual access to the media, he had the opportunity to connect with the public. He framed the issue as a battle between compassionate government officials and cold-hearted budget cutters. Clinton talked frequently of the need to protect senior citizens who could not afford to pay increased medical costs and of the need to protect programs for the poor and the young. He depicted his Republican critics as being irresponsible in their proposed budget cuts by being more interested in cutting taxes then helping Americans in need of assistance.

President Clinton also accentuated the positive in his speeches about the budget. The message that he wanted Americans to hear was that, as president, he had already been cutting the deficit and that he had reversed a trend to increase the budget deficit on an annual basis. Clinton also pointed with pride to an improving economy with falling interest rates and economic growth in many sectors. He told the American people that he was prepared to decrease the deficit by reducing federal expenditures, but he would not do so by dramatically slashing funding for programs like Medicare, Medicaid, aid to education, and projects to protect the environment.

Framing the issues is crucial in communicating with the public. Quite often, when I have experienced difficulty, it has been because I have allowed other people to define the issues and my position rather than defining the issues myself.

Like President Clinton, I was encountering massive opposition concerning any possible budget increase. My first step was to work with the school board. The school board was already being barraged by citizens outraged over the high cost of a Westborough education. Under intense pressure from the community and the school board, I did twice move in directions that I would later regret, for I allowed others to frame the debate.

My first step in budget building with the school board was to set priorities which would help in determining what would be included in the budget. This is a sound approach to getting the school board and the superintendent in agreement in advance of the formal budget deliberations. At a meeting held in my office prior to budget formulation, the school board established the following budget priorities:

Priority 1: Establish class sizes as follows:
- Grades kindergarten to three, eighteen to twenty-two students
- Grades four to six, twenty to twenty-three students
- Grades seven and eight, twenty-two to twenty-four students
- Grades nine to twelve, as many students as currently exist in the high school

I assured the committee that class size was not my highest priority as I believed that class size, although very important, could prove so costly that it could make other priorities such as teacher training or needed support services unattainable. I pointed out how in California and Florida, state laws limiting class size had put a stranglehold on other needed educational items and was proving extremely costly. However, the school board deeply believed in the need for this priority, and I saw it as a way to get them to agree to the budget, so I acquiesced.

The decision to make class size the first priority proved poor judgment on my part. Although it won school board support for limiting staff cuts and was very popular with parents, it would limit me in future budget development. It made class size appear to be the backbone of success in our system, and I did not believe that. I knew some outstanding school systems that did not have low class sizes but had proved very effective because of innovation and outstanding staff-development programs. However, by endorsing class size as the critical element, I was giving it a priority that would hamper the school system in developing future budgets.

Priority 2: Evaluate current protocols for monitoring the academic, social, and emotional health of all students and recommend improvements. To this day I am not sure what that means. However, the school board saw this as a way "to stop students from falling between the cracks." To me, it was hard to be against it, so it became a priority without much discussion.

Priority 3: Explore additional revenue generation options. Here the school board was interested in seeing if the school system could become more entrepreneurial, and that appeared to make sense.

Priority 4: Explore cost-saving options. This is certainly a legitimate priority for any budget.

The school board did caution me emphatically to present a budget that was sellable to the town. They expressed the view that this was an unusually difficult year due to the decrease in state and local receipts advised me to exercise fiscal restraint in developing a budget. Here, I made my second error in judgment.

I spent hours agonizing over my recommendation for the bottom line of the budget. The three figures that I considered were a 7.5 percent increase, which would allow us to expand programs, a 4.5 percent increase, which would allow us to maintain what we had with built-in increases for rising salaries and fixed costs, and a 0 percent increase, which constituted level funding and would require us to cut back on services. I decided on 0 percent (actually the exact figure was 0.3 percent less than zero) because I did not see how, politically, any higher budget could win the approval of the town. Local property taxes had jumped almost 20 percent in the previous two-year period, and I did not believe there was any chance that the public would agree to an increase of that magnitude again. Even with a 0 percent increase, taxes were projected to go up another 9 percent.

In hindsight, I now realize that I should have gone through the process of requesting what I needed to maintain the excellence of the Westborough school system. There would be many opportunities for me to work with the school board to lower the budget during the process, so it was not like my budget numbers would have been set in stone. Instead, I developed a budget with an eye more on the school board and the finances of the town than on the needs of the students. This was not a terrible thing as my strategy was to have an affordable budget on which I could get support from the school board and from the voters. Still, I lowballed my own budget in an attempt to work out a compromise. A sounder strategy would have been to state what I needed in the budget and then agree to the school board's lowering the budget to meet the financial needs of the town.

Once I agreed to this bottom-line figure, the pressure was on to show how I would make this work. With the help of my special education director, we reorganized special education by adding additional programs. Although this mandated a higher level of special education staffing, it allowed us to recoup savings by keeping more students in the district rather than sending them to out-of-district placements. This was a win for the district and for the students. It would allow us to keep our students in Westborough to be educated with their friends and neighbors while at the same time reducing tuition and transportation costs.

Another positive initiative was expanding our community education program. This involved increasing the number of existing programs in child care, after-school extracurricular activities for elementary school students, and adult education. We projected raising about $300,000 in his area.

The third revenue generator was by far the most controversial. With great reluctance, I included in my budget a provision for athletic and extracurricular fees at the secondary level, which would generate almost $200,000 in revenue. Although I have always opposed fees, I considered this a better course of action than reducing services. The fee provision provoked an argument with certain school board members as they preferred a transportation fee or, better yet, no fees at all. Their logic was that an athletic fee would prevent some of the students who needed them most from participating in the athletic programs. I did not agree and felt a bus fee was punitive as it required students to pay to get to school to get an education, while an athletic fee only required payment for an extracurricular activity. My reasoning to them was that parents already pay fees for sports in the town, so this would merely be an extension of that practice. I also assured them that needy students would be able to secure fee waivers to participate. Even with my best arguments presented, the school board did not like the concept of fees for activities. Finally, with the school board it came down to my saying, "It's fees or the reduction of five additional teachers," so they reluctantly bought into the fees.

I also included no salary increase in the budget as we were still negotiating with the teachers. Doing this allowed me to bring a 0 percent increase forward for teacher raises, which proved close to the actual negotiated figure. Still, even with the enhanced revenue from athletic fees and from community education, the budget proposal involved the reduction of thirteen teaching positions. Given the lack of community support, bringing this austere budget forward may well have been the right thing to do politically, but I have always felt badly about this decision. What also bothered me afterward was the realization that parents looked to me to give them an honest budget. Coming in initially at zero sent the message that the superintendent felt we could make do for the next year without an increase and yet maintain the same services and results.

Advocating for the Budget

President Bill Clinton found himself in a continuing debate with Representative Newt Gingrich and Republican leadership during the summer of 1995. Clinton wanted to maintain strong programs in health care, education, and the environment through federal support for these programs, while Gingrich and many Republicans sought to turn over these programs to the states in the form of block grants, federal money given to the states to maintain these programs according to federal guidelines.

The talks between Clinton and Gingrich moved slowly throughout the summer. President Clinton always kept the message clear. Clinton emphasized that his role as president was to protect the interests of all Americans, especially those who might not be able to protect themselves, such as the poor, the young, and the elderly. He maintained his position even when warned by Newt Gingrich that the country was moving toward "a train wreck." Both Clinton and Gingrich knew that midnight of September 30 was a drop-dead date for a new budget, as October 1 began the new federal fiscal year. If no budget or special appropriations bill was passed by that date, only a continuing resolution from Congress would allow the government the money it needed to remain functioning.

A continuous resolution was passed on September 28. The resolution allowed the government to spend at the same levels as in the previous budget through November 13. However, although the "train wreck" was delayed due to continual disagreements between the president and the Republican congressional leadership, the government was eventually forced to close twice, once for six days and once for twenty-one days. The shutdown meant that essential services, such as defense, law enforcement, and the processing of Social Security checks, would continue, but nonessential services would be cut. Many government offices, national parks, museums, and laboratories were all shutdown as there was no money to support them.

The public was outraged at the shutdown. People wanted government service, and they felt sympathy for the federal workers who were not receiving paychecks. The people blamed Representative Gingrich for the fiasco. Even some fellow Republicans felt Gingrich's leadership was reckless. Clinton continued his focus, and he faulted Gingrich and the Republicans for not supporting reasonable funding for federal programs. Newt Gingrich knew he had overplayed his hand, and eventually, on April 24, 1996, a budget was finally approved by Congress that greatly moderated Gingrich's proposed reductions.

Like President Clinton, I needed a message to sell the budget. Even with the 0 percent increase, there was still great opposition to the budget because of the escalating property taxes. To my critics, even a 0 percent school budget increase was too much as it still meant a projected local property tax increase of 9 percent. The finance committee was still looking for about $750,000 in additional cuts to win their endorsement. Like President Clinton, I would rather not compromise than make cuts that drastic. I was already cutting thirteen classroom teaching positions. To cut another $750,000 could be the equivalent of cutting almost twenty additional teachers. Our best option was to take our budget to town meeting, knowing that without the endorsement of the finance committee there would be formidable opposition from those who viewed the school department as arrogant and uncompromising.

We knew our best hope for budget approval would be to have the parents of school-age children attend the town meeting, which began in Westborough on the first Saturday afternoon in May and usually extended another two or three days, depending on the number and complexity of the articles that had to be addressed. This would be difficult as parents tend to want to spend Saturday afternoons in the spring with their children, and town meeting always takes up the school budget on a Saturday. In addition, for many parents, child care is a big challenge. Even if parents wanted to come and support the school budget at town meeting, they still needed to have child care. We would have to plan carefully in this area.

The first step in developing support for the budget was to set out a clear, simple message. "We need it because we've always had it" is not a message designed to garner the enthusiasm and support of the community. Many of the town's people were still angry over continuing tax increases, so the administration had to send a compelling message.

We decided on a message that was simple: the Westborough Public Schools provides a superior education for its children, and the schools need adequate resources to maintain this level of quality. We also talked about how many people had moved to Westborough because of the schools and how the schools were what had driven up the value of the homes in the town. Our College Board scores and state testing scores are always high, we stressed, and the programs we provided for all students were of excellent quality. We also emphasized that for four years in a row, our music program had won national recognition as being one of the top hundred in the country. Over and over, we talked of the quality of Westborough schools. When we were challenged to explain how other towns could do almost as well with smaller budgets, we discussed the fact that many people had moved to Westborough because they wanted the best. We were providing the extras, such as outstanding music and special education programs, which were very expensive to maintain. Also, our small class sizes allowed for more individual attention, and class size was one of the most costly elements in the budget. The message was clear: staying at the top would cost money.

Once the message was clearly delineated, we used the media, mailings, public meetings, and home visits to key neighborhoods to explain why we needed the requested budget. There was a perception that as we had high per-pupil expenditure, we could afford to take a cut and still provide the same level of quality. We stressed that our 0 percent increase in the budget showed our willingness to respond to the difficult financial condition of the town. We also presented a scenario of exactly what our cuts would mean to the students and what the impact of the additional reductions requested by the finance committee would be. Interestingly, these forums proved very easy as only school supporters would come, not school critics. Soon, there was a critical mass of supporters organizing for the confrontation at town meeting. I also met with the staff at each school, as well as had a general staff meeting. My message was clear to them: we needed approval of this budget, or there would be more dramatic cuts. Teachers who are town residents and their families were encouraged to attend the town meeting to support the budget.

We were well organized for the town meeting showdown with our critics. Our position had been clearly stated through meetings and written material. One member of the school board had even compiled the e-mail addresses of the parents and had sent out several messages to them reminding them of the importance of town meeting and giving them the date and time. In addition, we advertised that baby-sitting would be available during the town meeting session no matter how late the meeting ran. The baby-sitting would extend through the entire town meeting and not just during the time for the school board budget as we did not want to be accused of unfairly packing the audience with supportive parents.

The day of town meeting, the auditorium was packed with voters. Both the chair and I presented the budget to the assembly. As we presented, parents, who were watching on television, began to fill the overflow rooms as there were no more seats in the auditorium. In addition, a group of parents formed a cell phone brigade to call other parents whom they did not see at town meeting. The swell of late arrivals pushed us over the top. With nine hundred voters present, the school budget won by only forty votes.

Results

With the approval of the federal budget in April 1996, President Clinton won big in his fight with Representative Newt Gingrich and Congress. He did get a budget that he believed would meet the needs of the country, and he did show strength and resolve as president. Bill Clinton won a huge political victory as many voters perceived him to be a leader willing to stand up for his beliefs. He was to be rewarded at the polls. During the election of 1998, not only did Clinton win by a large majority, but the Democrats gained an increase of eight seats in Congress, reversing the "Gingrich revolution," which had portrayed the Democrats as out of touch with the people.

In Westborough, we lived with a difficult budget in 2005, which still was not nearly as bad as it would have been if we had lost at town meeting. Class sizes did increase dramatically at the high school level, and programs were reduced at the middle school level, which demonstrated to people in the town that budget cuts do impact education. However, budgeting for the following year became much less acrimonious as both sides wished to avoid the controversy of the previous year. Our critics also knew that the school could still get the vote out and would not concede easily, even during challenging times. That next year we received almost a 5 percent increase, which helped the schools restore lower class sizes at the high school.

At all times, there will be many reasons presented by critics to cut the budget. The superintendent is the spokesman for the children, and it is his responsibility to develop a plan and advocate for the needed funding. It is the responsibility of the school board and the voters to determine if the plan should be implemented.

Reflection Points

- Budget for what you need to maintain the standards of your system. Compromises may be necessary, but the school committee and the community should know from the superintendent's perspective what the system needs.

- Do not allow others to frame the budget issues. As superintendent, you are in the best position to make budget decisions. Make it clear to the public what needs to be done. Also, keep instruction as the priority of the budget.
- Accentuate the positive during the budget process. Describe to people how tax money is spent in order to provide quality programs. Emphasize how results have demonstrated that money has been well spent. The public is always concerned about accountability. In their view, additional money must translate into improvement.
- Keep budget information flowing throughout the process. Keep presentations simple. Visuals such as charts and graphs are helpful. Critics of the budget will certainly be providing information.
- Present scenarios of what will happen if the budget is reduced. Scenarios should be specific enough that parents will know exactly how the cutbacks will effect their children.
- Keep staff informed about the budget. Not only can staff members who live in town help at town meeting, but they also serve as key communicators to their friends and neighbors in the community.
- Never apologize for your budget. The superintendent's job is to advocate for children.

Afterword

As a former superintendent of schools, how many times did I reflect on presidential precedents while I made my decisions? The answer is, as many times as I thought about the properties of benzene, the appropriate applications of the quadratic formula, or the achievements of Otto of Wittlesbach. Realistically, I never consciously thought of historical precedents in difficult situations; nor should I have. Reflection does not work in this manner. Rather, reflection links all relevant prior experiences and acquired knowledge to solve an existing problem. Reflection uses the mind as an idea processor to determine action. In this book, I used historical examples because they are meaningful to me, and history is one element that has shaped who I am and how I act. In addition to history, my religion, family, education, friendships, and professional experiences are just some of the factors that form the gestalt of what influences me to act in a certain way. Like you, I face difficult situations, which put pressure on me and make decision making more difficult. I recommend that you continually reflect on lessons from your past experiences. I also urge you to discuss important issues with your fellow superintendents. They also have experiences that they can reflect on to advise you. You can then integrate their wisdom into your knowledge base.

It would be helpful if we could isolate issues and just do things the same way Eisenhower, Kennedy, or some other successful leader did once before. However, you and I have had different experiences than Kennedy or Eisenhower. Their decisions are frozen in time. We have to reflect on our own personal experience and knowledge and apply them to our present conditions. I would urge all administrators and aspiring administrators to partake in as many learning experiences as possible to develop a database of the mind that is filled with rich learning experiences. I would also urge administrators to read as much as possible in order to add new perspectives, which will enhance reflection. Reading management books will certainly allow you to learn new strategies and techniques that will be helpful to you as a superintendent. These books help you understand how organizations work. Just as importantly, I urge the study of the humanities and social science as those disciplines help explain how people act. Reading, experience, and meaningful discussions will expand your database of knowledge for reflection.

Being the superintendent of schools is a fast-paced and rewarding profession. I have enjoyed it and feel I have made a difference. I am now an educational and business consultant. This book has allowed me to reflect on my career through the mirror of history, and these reflections will allow me to guide younger administrators in their thinking. I would hope that this book has given you a perspective on reflection and will prove of value to you in administering your school system.

Resources

Books

Beschloss, M., ed. 2002. *Reaching for glory: Lyndon Johnson's secret White House tapes, 1964–65.* New York: Simon and Schuster.

Bush, G., and B. Scowcroft. 1998. *A world transformed.* New York: Knopf.

Carter, J. 1982. *Keeping faith: Memoirs of a president.* New York: Bantam Books.

Clinton, B. 2004. *My life.* New York: Knopf.

Dallek, R. 1996 *Hail to the chief: The making and unmaking of American presidents.* New York: Hyperion.

———. 1998. *Flawed giant: Lyndon Johnson and his times, 1961–1973.* New York: Oxford University Press.

———. 2003. *An unfinished life: John F. Kennedy, 1917–1963.* Boston: Little, Brown.

Drew, E. 1996. *Showdown: The struggle between the Gingrich Congress and the Clinton White House.* New York: Simon & Schuster.

Eisenhower, D. 1965[1963]. *Mandate for change: The White House Years, 1953–1956.* New York: New American Library.

Goodwin, D. K. 1976. *Lyndon Johnson and the American dream.* New York: Harper & Row.

Greenstein, F. I. 1994. *The hidden-hand presidency: Eisenhower as a leader.* Baltimore: Johns Hopkins University Press.

Harris, J. F. 2005. *The survivor: Bill Clinton in the White House.* New York: Random House.

Halberstram, D. 1993. *The fifties.* New York: Villard Books.

Kissinger, H. 1994. *Diplomacy.* New York: Simon & Schuster.

Manchester, W. R. 1978. *American Caesar, Douglas MacArthur, 1880–1964.* Boston: Little, Brown.

———. 1974. *The glory and the dream: A narrative history of America, 1932–1972.* New York: Bantam Books.

Matlock, J. F., Jr. 2004. *Reagan and Gorbachev: How the cold war ended.* New York: Random House.

McCullough, D. 1993. *Truman.* New York: Simon & Schuster.

Morris, E. 1999. *Dutch: A memoir of Ronald Reagan.* New York: Modern Library.

Oates, Stephen, P. 1982. *Let the trumpet sound: The life of Martin Luther King, Jr.* New York: Harper & Row.

Patterson, J. T. 1996. *Great expectations: The United States, 1945–74.* New York: Oxford University Press.

Quandt, W. B. 1986. *Camp David: Peacemaking and politics.* Washington, D.C.: Brookings Institute.

Redmon, C. 1986. *Come as you are: The Peace Corps story.* New York: Harcourt Brace Jovanovich.

Reeves, R. 1993. *President Kennedy: Profile of power.* New York: Simon & Schuster.

Schlesinger, A. M., Jr. 1956. *The age of Roosevelt: The crisis of the old order, 1919–1933.* Boston: Houghton Mifflin.

———. 1965. *A thousand days: John Kennedy in the White House.* Boston: Houghton Mifflin.

Smith, J. E. 1992. *George Bush's war.* New York: Holt.

Sorenson, T. C. 1965. *Kennedy.* New York: Harper & Row.

Troy, G. 2005. *Morning in America: How Ronald Reagan invented the 80s.* Princeton, N.J.: Princeton University Press.

Wofford, H. 1980. *Of Kennedy and kings: Making sense of the sixties.* Pittsburgh, PA: University of Pittsburgh Press.

Films

Kamen, R. M. (writer), J. G. Avildsen (producer), and J. Weintraub (director). 1987. *The Karate Kid* [videorecording]. Burbank, CA: Columbia Pictures.

Web pages

"Christopher Columbus Discovers America, 1492," *Eyewitness to History,* available at www.eyewitnesstohistory.com/columbus.htm (last accessed January 19, 2005).

Kennedy, J. F., "Radio and Television Report to the American People on the Berlin Crisis, July 25, 1961," available at www.jfklibrary.org/Historical+ Resources/Archives/Reference+Desk/Speeches/JFK/003POF03Berlin Crisis07251961.htm (last accessed November 5, 2004).

Peace Corps, "Life Is Calling. How Far Will You Go?" available at www.peacecorps.org (last accessed August 20, 2004).

"President Lyndon B. Johnson Described As Greatest Civil Rights President," available at www.galenet.galegroup.com (last accessed December 22, 2004).

About the Author

Stephen Dlott served as a school administrator for over thirty years. Before retiring in July of 2005, he served the Westborough Public Schools for sixteen years: as superintendent for nine years and as an assistant superintendent for eight additional years. Previous to that, he was a high school administrator for fourteen years: eleven years as principal and three years as assistant principal.